GARDEN
features and ornament

David Stevens

conran
OCTOPUS

First published in 1999 by
Conran Octopus Limited
37 Shelton Street
London WC2H 9HN
a part of Octopus Publishing Group

Text copyright © David Stevens, 1995, 1999
Design and layout copyright © Conran Octopus Limited 1995, 1999

Material in this book was originally featured in The Garden Design Sourcebook, published in 1995 by Conran Octopus Limited.

ISBN 1 84091 050 X

Illustrations by Vanessa Luff

Art Editors Tony Seddon, Amanda Lerwill
Project Editors Kate Bell, Tanya Robinson
Picture Research Nadine Bazar, Julia Pashley, Rachel Davies
Illustration Visualization Lesley Craig
Production Julia Golding, Julian Deeming

Printed in Hong Kong

CONTENTS

On the first fine day of spring there is frequently a stirring within gardeners – an excitement caused by the expectancy of the season to come, which can lead to an overwhelming desire to start anew.

Caught up in such a surge of enthusiasm, it is all too easy to rush to the nearest nursery and buy a series of disparate elements, before heading home again to position them in your garden in a frenzy of disorganization. Apart from resulting in artless chaos, this approach is needlessly expensive and is the complete antithesis of sound design – it leads only to over-complication, which spells disaster in any garden.

Good design is characterized by simplicity, strength of purpose and a unity of overall theme. Yet this does not necessarily imply a lack of interest or bland minimalism; great gardens, large or small, can be enormously subtle, packed with interest and, above all, exciting.

The bones of any garden composition are provided by the hard landscape structure of paving, walls and paths, as well as lawns, ground cover areas and planted borders.

But within these can be woven all kinds of incidentals. Some, such as rock outcrops, are major features which draw the eye and need careful positioning. Overhead structures, on the other hand, provide an upper limit to a garden, a ceiling that defines vertical space while often, as in the case of pergolas, encouraging movement through the area in a particular direction.

Furniture and ornament are also key components, providing points of interest that can either be displayed in full view or 'happened upon' as you turn a corner or enter each different garden room. Your choice of furniture and ornament, however, will need careful thought as it is easy to become overly complicated. But when handled deftly, they can express individuality and help set one garden apart from another, making it your own personal space.

The rule of simplicity suggests that major features should be limited in number, depending, of course, on the size of the garden. A small space,

Left: *This individualistic water feature creates both sound and movement, but must link with the overall garden theme beyond to avoid ostentation.*

Above: *This superb composition certainly qualifies as an outdoor room. Floors, walls and ceilings can be furnished and clothed in an infinite number of ways.*

therefore, might have room for only one, but where the plot is of ample size, or sub-divided, it often makes sense to have one in each area, so that each can be glimpsed from the preceding space to beckon you onwards.

The positioning of any feature will have a direct impact on the way a garden design works in visual terms. A real eye-catcher placed at the bottom of a long narrow space demands attention: it dominates the entire area and draws the eye, foreshortening the garden by forcing you to ignore things elsewhere.

If, on the other hand, the same feature is positioned to one side, just over half way down the garden, you now have the potential to open the pattern of the space on a diagonal. As diagonals are the longest dimensions available within a rectangle, it is possible to increase the feeling of space. Also, it is worth keeping in mind that one feature in the distance can be counter-balanced by something smaller in the foreground. This becomes the basis of informal asymmetrical design – a theme that can be developed throughout the rest of the space.

Formality, on the other hand, depends on similar features being balanced by one another and placed in regular positions within the garden. On a large scale this could be two pavilions or pools, while on a more intimate scale, it might simply be two carefully positioned pots or urns on either side of a doorway or flight of steps.

Another important consideration is the implications your choice will have on subsequent construction. For example, if a pool has a formal outline, it will sit comfortably within an architectural area of the garden, quite possibly adjoining the house, within crisp, well-detailed paving. An informal space, on the other hand, suggests free-form shapes that will blend into the more distant parts of the composition. The construction of both of these features will entail using a tough butyl liner, but the best way of concealing the edges will depend entirely on the unique characteristics of your garden. This in turn will have an impact on the cost of the project, which for many is a crucial concern.

In other words, a successful garden is the sum of all its features and furnishings. It is these different elements which bring the space alive in a way that is entirely personal.

Left: *Ironwork normally has a delicate pattern that blends well with a planted background. Colour too is important: white stands out while black becomes nearly invisible.*

KEY TO SYMBOLS

COST

| cheap | medium-priced | expensive |

EASE OF USE

| straightforward | moderate | complicated |

DURABILITY

| short-term | medium-term | long-term |

Above: *Pergolas and tunnels really frame a view, drawing you down their length with a delicious feeling of anticipation. Here the movement is accentuated by the beds of lavender, which focus on the gate, which in turn leads to the meadow beyond.*

While we accept that floors and walls are essential parts of a garden, we often ignore the potential of the ceiling to transform the character of a garden.

There are many overhead features, not the least of which are trees, that help to contain and define vertical space. These are useful tools that lead us through the garden, provide screening from intrusive views and unwelcome onlookers, and are focal points in their own right. Most of us are familiar with pergolas, arches and overhead beams, yet frequently forget about arbours, fruit tunnels and even awnings. When these major features are included, they are all too often plonked down at random, with no thought for their relationship with the surrounding world.

To use any feature successfully involves an understanding of what it can achieve, which requires an appreciation of garden design principles. The secret of siting and using any feature is to let the situation dictate the device. Pergolas, arches and tunnels will positively draw you through a space, which in turn suggests the next rule, that these same features must lead somewhere. There is no point in designing and building a fine pergola that leads, as so often happens, straight to the compost heap or shed!

A common denominator for any pergola, arch or tunnel is the ability to provide the essential design ingredients of tension, mystery and surprise. As you approach a feature, your curiosity about what is waiting beyond creates a tension and sense of expectancy. As you emerge into a different part of the garden, surprise is followed by a release of tension. Each feature, however, handles this tension in a different way. An arch is quickly negotiated while a pergola takes longer to explore and tempts you with glimpses of the garden to either side. A tunnel is the most dramatic, a shadowy path that insulates you before providing a tantalising view of what lies ahead, and into which you will burst on exit. No matter how fleeting the journey, it is essential that both ends are carefully positioned to ensure that the drama from either direction is worth the wait.

Static features, like overhead structures and arbours, attract in a different way, drawing you towards them. Overhead structures are essentially an extension of the house, or any other building, while arbours will normally be positioned in a more distant part of the garden, as a positive focal point. To be successful, both overhead structures and arbours should reflect the style of their surroundings, otherwise they may jar with the garden and look incongruous.

Awnings also need siting with consideration for their environment. Transient and colourful, they can be rolled out above a terrace, simply cast over beams or even spread amongst the branches of a tree to provide shade and shelter wherever it is needed. This kind of informality can loosen up your attitude to living outside, encouraging you to roam freely about the garden and use different places to sit, dine or entertain.

Overall, it is of prime importance that you choose and site major structures keeping the overall style and character of the garden firmly in mind. It is always a good idea to keep in mind that understatement is invariably more successful than showing-off – a philosophy as apt for gardens as it is for people. In addition, never slavishly copy ideas for a major garden feature straight from a book, these will invariably look awkward in your own garden. Instead, remember that your garden, like your clothes, should suit you.

Opposite: *Overhead structures define vertical space, providing a ceiling to the area they cover. Apart from casting shade, they offer the perfect support for climbing plants. The design, construction and choice of materials should be sympathetic to other features in the garden.*

Above: *While this delicate metal arch hardly disturbs the view, it just suggests a pause, halfway down the path. The 'walls' of the hedge lead the eye onwards to what lies beyond.*

Right: *This minimal structure contributes to an overall visual lightness while providing gently dappled shade. Such an approach is in direct contrast to a heavier structure, where enclosure is the most important factor.*

METAL ARCHES

Metal arches are simply vehicles for climbing plants, their delicacy of line and visual lightness allowing for minimal disruption to the overall scene. Hoops are often wired together, allowing climbers to scramble over the structure.

Characteristics: Metal has long been used for arches and pergolas, and its strength and durability make it an obvious choice. It is possible to achieve great delicacy of design, and you will see beautifully detailed and elaborate wrought-iron designs in many historic gardens. The downside is the cost, and the need for a skilled metal worker to do the work.

Wrought iron can be worked by hand to virtually any pattern, whereas cast iron – popular with the Victorians as a cheap alternative – was only available in set patterns. Cast-iron arches and pergolas can still be found at auction, but be careful as they are brittle, and if broken, virtually impossible to repair. Remarkably effective, simple designs can also be constructed from bent pipework, and I have seen superb purpose-built arches constructed from plumbing fittings. Oxidized copper, in particular, looks stunning, especially when covered with climbers. Bent mild steel rods, too, can be used, and will produce a very light effect. The structure is held together with galvanized wire, and if painted black will settle into the background. (Be sure to avoid the overworked thin white wire contraptions like the plague; they look dreadful.) Plastic-coated tubing is popular, has a long life, and comes in an alarming range of patterns, but the simpler shapes are acceptable, especially if you allow climbers to soften and detract from the structure.

Uses: Metal arches have a lightness and delicacy that makes them ideal hosts for delicate climbers that would be dominated by heavier structures.

Construction/erection: The older types usually had some kind of 'feet' that were surrounded by rammed soil or concreted in position. Concrete is the best fixing for modern arches.

Contrasting & associating materials: Depending on the style and materials chosen, they will easily blend into traditional or modern compositions.

This simple hoop makes the most charming and informal arch, and is used to span this walkway, linking the two delightfully planted borders together. A timber arch would have been far too heavy here, whereas metal makes an ideal choice.

WOODEN ARCHES

Timber is the most versatile material at the garden designer's disposal, and this combination of a sturdy framework, laced with a delicate trellis, emphasizes the point perfectly. The picket gate cleverly echoes the curve of the arch.

Characteristics: Arches are strong vertical elements that demand attention, and will form important punctuation points in a garden. Timber is the most common material used for their construction, and the easiest to handle. Styles vary enormously, from very basic affairs with just two uprights and a cross-member, to complex designs using all kinds of woodwork, struts and patterning. However, as with most things in the garden, the simpler things work best, and unless there is a very good reason for a complicated design (possibly to match the overall composition), arches are best kept simple. They should also be compatible with any adjoining divider or boundary, and either painted, or stained using a suitable non-toxic preservative.

Uses: Arches must be planned as an integral part of the garden design. They can be used to frame a path, link dividers, emphasize the entrance to a new garden room, or to act as a specific point of emphasis when entering the plot from the street.

Construction: This will be straightforward or complicated, according to the design. Simple arches can often be bought in kit form, and either concreted into the ground or set in spiked metal shoes. More complex designs are best built by a carpenter and assembled on site.

Contrasting & associating materials: As an arch should reflect the overall style of the garden, it should blend into, rather than contrast with its immediate surroundings.

WOVEN ARCHES

Woven osiers can be used to create a structure that has far greater flexibility than the more usual split-hazel wattles. This example sits comfortably among informal planting; climbers can be wired in position or allowed to twine naturally in with the weave.

Characteristics: Woven stems are a traditional garden material, and woven osiers (willow stems), reed or bamboo – all more flexible than the split hazel used for wattles – can be used to make arches and arbours to match the overall character of the garden. All these materials have a relatively short life, and you should expect them to last no more than eight or ten years. There is also the problem of squirrels which, in certain areas, seem to take delight in eating them. I have seen an entire arch, as well as woven figures, all made from osiers, disappear in this way in the space of two years.

Uses: Features such as these can be used in a wide range of settings, perhaps adjoining fencing made of similar material.

Construction: You will need a skilled craftsman, of which there are still a surprisingly large number. Weavers often display their work at county and rural craft shows. Features of this kind must be securely anchored to prevent them from being blown away in a high wind. The best method is to use bent wire spikes, which are much like tent pegs, threaded through the lower weave and driven firmly into the ground.

Contrasting & associating materials: Features made from these materials associate well with a wide range of other natural materials such as timber and stone, and look handsome set against and among planting. They go well with fencing made of the same material, or with woven garden furniture.

BRICK & STONE ARCHES

Characteristics: These are the most permanent members of the breed, almost always built as part of a boundary wall, major dividing wall, or adjoining a house or outbuilding. Where an arch pierces a wall, the solidity of the wall itself will give it additional punctuation power, while the addition of a gate or door will further increase the tension and expectancy of what lies beyond.

It is possible to mix brick and stone, and because brick is more easily worked than the latter, and forms a cleaner profile into which a door or gate frame can be fitted, you will often see a beautifully detailed brick arch set in a stone wall. The shape of a brick or stone arch can vary considerably; each – whether semicircular, pointed, flat or ogee – will contribute a different emphasis, and should always be determined by the overall style of the garden.

It is essential that a brick or stone arch is built as an integral part of the garden design. A poorly conceived arch of this kind can smack of the worst suburbanism. Arches built of a single thickness of brick, or of imitation stonework, tacked on to the house for no good reason, or self-consciously rising above a low boundary wall, perhaps with a flimsy wrought-iron gate, should be avoided at all costs. Not only will these lack visual stability, but a misdirected

knock with a heavily laden wheelbarrow can often damage them beyond repair – perhaps the best fate!

Uses: As a major focal point and means of access through a boundary or internal dividing wall. Such arches demand attention, and positively draw both feet and eye towards them. This means that you can often highlight the area still further, perhaps by adding urns or fastigiate planting to either side.

Construction: As arches normally form part of a boundary or dividing wall, they will usually be built by a bricklayer or mason. The shape will be formed by a wooden template or turning piece, which is fixed into place to allow the brick or stonework to be built around it. Once the arch is completed, the turning piece will be removed. The wider the arch, the more complicated it is to construct.

Contrasting & associating materials: An arch must be entirely compatible with the wall in which it is set; both will be major elements in the garden as a whole. Brick walls and arches associate best with brick paving, stone with stone; both can be softened by planting. Where there is a mix of materials, such as brick and stone, then the dominant partner should link with similar materials.

Stone not only provides enormous structural and visual strength, but quickly acquires a patina of age that will settle it comfortably into the surrounding garden. This series of arches provides a powerful perspective that is effectively terminated by the carefully placed statue.

METAL PERGOLAS

There is a strong affinity between this metal pergola and the vine climbing over it as the twisted branches of the latter are virtually the same thickness as the smooth metal arches. Such a complementary visual dialogue forms the perfect garden feature.

Characteristics: The obvious advantages of metal over timber are its durability and strength. The strength of metal makes it possible to use thinner elements, so that the pergola can become a virtually invisible support for planting allowed to float over the surface.

Traditional examples, however, used a heavier gauge of metal, which was often worked into superb designs. Most were made of wrought iron, though some were cast and are therefore more brittle. I often find wonderful ones tucked away in neglected gardens, in various states of decay but always worth repairing.

One of the best contemporary examples I have seen was constructed from plumbing pipes and fittings. These allow a straightforward framework of uprights and overheads, with the added advantage that the overheads can readily be bent to form an arc. An excellent example of lateral thinking, in which the materials of one trade are used for quite a different discipline. I myself have built some wonderful hooped pergolas in large-diameter pipework, painted in bright primary colours.

You can, of course, buy plastic-coated tubular metal for the purpose. While the simplest and most readily available shapes are just about acceptable, those that fall into the trap of 'design for design's sake' certainly are not. No pergola, unless very carefully conceived and positioned, should aim to be a scene-stealer in its own right.

Uses: All pergolas are there for the purpose of supporting plants, and metal ones are less visually intrusive than timber ones.

Construction: Traditional examples often had a shoe, or bent metal section, incorporated at the bottom of each leg. This was firmly bedded in soil, or concreted into position, and provided virtually indestructible strength. Newer examples can be bought in kit form and slotted together. The vertical poles are either simply set in the ground (when they may not prove strong enough in a gale, once they are covered in plants), or concreted in. Fine mesh plastic can be stretched and tied over the whole structure to allow climbers to get an easy toe-hold.

Repairs to antique pergolas can often be carried out by a welder, and will probably need to be done on site.

Contrasting & associating materials: Traditional metal pergolas will blend into virtually any setting. Contemporary versions look great in the modern world. Modern plastic-coated affairs, which look pretty bland, look fine in bland gardens!

WOODEN PERGOLAS

The appearance of a timber pergola can be transformed by an application of paint. This eye-catching and vibrant structure, designed by Jill Billington, forms a striking focal point. The architectural line is emphasized by the crisp slate paving and the adjacent planting.

Characteristics: A pergola, a continuous series of arches, is essentially a vehicle for the plants grown over it and should always play second fiddle to the foliage and flowers of climbers and other associated planting. A pergola should be an integral part of the hard landscape framework of the garden, never an ostentatious addition. Timber (and less frequently, metal) is traditionally used, though you will also see brick or stone piers spanned by wooden beams. Many beautifully detailed examples of such pergolas can be found in historic gardens but never confuse impeccable detailing with fussy ornamentation; the two things are quite separate, and should remain so!

The flimsy rustic pergola of bark-covered larch poles is not only visually feeble, but will soon deteriorate; bark should always be removed from any structure as it traps water and encourages rot. However, this type of structure should not be confused with the round-pole pergolas and overhead features found throughout the Mediterranean, which are delightful, and very much part of a local vernacular style.

Uses: The purpose of a pergola is as a support which will allow climbing plants to be seen at their best, as well as a linking element between different parts of the garden.

Construction: Simplicity of design is important, and this means sound construction, using timber of generous proportions for both uprights and cross-beams. Hardwoods, such as oak, are especially suitable for outdoor wooden structures, and will last for many years, though softwoods, provided they are pressure-treated before purchase, or regularly treated with a non-toxic preservative, can also be used. Timber uprights can either be concreted into the ground, with the concrete brought just above ground level and slightly chamfered to shed water easily, or set into metal shoes that are driven into position before construction starts. Brick or stone piers will provide great durability and strength.

Planting will need unobtrusive support, particularly when training young plants, and wires can be neatly threaded through metal eyes screwed into the uprights and cross-beams.

Contrasting & associating materials: Timber associates well with brick or stone flooring, and brick or stone piers will allow the flooring material to be extended upwards, providing vertical continuity. A timber pergola will sit comfortably with timber trellis, which can be used to infill individual sections or to act as an extension, running out from the main structure and blending the line out into the wider garden.

PERGOLAS

Trellis was once a traditional material for constructing pergolas, giving the overall structure great visual lightness. It is less often seen in use today, but provided the timber is generously proportioned and regularly treated against rot, it can last for years.

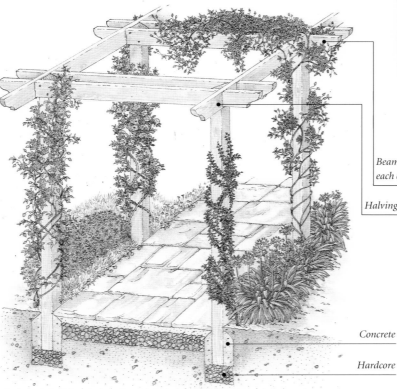

Beams may be shaped at
each end or left square

Halving joints

Concrete

Hardcore

When is a pergola not a pergola? The dividing line between an archway or arbour can be a narrow one. This is a delightful and practical structure that could be used as a host for a wide range of climbing plants.

DETAIL OF HALVING JOINTS

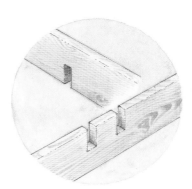

CONSTRUCTING A PERGOLA

Build pergolas using generously sized timbers to a design that is as sturdy as possible. Tie in climbers on to wires fixed both to the uprights and horizontals.

TUNNELS

Tunnels can play host to a wide range of planting, and while there are few vegetables that could do the job, climbing beans work perfectly, adding their vibrant flowers to the architectural foliage. Metal hoops are visually undemanding and when covered, are virtually invisible, allowing the maximum amount of light to filter through the planting.

Metal hoops are again used as the underlying structure of this tunnel, but the trees have grown together to form a dimly lit passage that has slightly mysterious and even sombre overtones. The fine statue at the far end of the walk provides a focus and naturally draws you down towards the sunlight at the end of the tunnel.

Characteristics: Tunnels seem inexplicably less popular than pergolas, yet they form delightful garden features and are not difficult to create. At their simplest, they need be little more than two parallel rows of hedge, trained to join at the top. They can be formed from yew or beech; from fruit trees, pleached limes and other trees; from willows plaited at the top; or, more informally, from trees planted in a narrow avenue with the canopy meeting at the top. Tunnels can be straight or curved, as space allows, and a curved tunnel will engender an enormous feeling of mystery as you wait for the view to open at the far end.

Uses: Tunnels may be used in much the same way as pergolas, but must have somewhere positive to go. They are particularly successful in linking two different areas of the garden, but remember that the view back is as important as the way forward. A formally clipped hedge will relate best to a formal composition, while a tunnel of trees could be perfect in less formal parts of the garden.

Planting: In many instances you will need a framework on to which to train the plants that form the tunnel. For fruit trees, you will need either posts and wires, or, more traditionally, wrought-iron hoops, over which the branches can be trained and tied. Limes and hornbeam can be tied into posts and wires, and the leaders trained over the top; willows are tied to stakes (also of willow), and carefully plaited as they grow. The stakes, incidentally, will almost always take root as well, and all species will need regular attention to keep the feature under control.

Contrasting & associating materials: This is a formal feature that looks best in an architectural garden setting or perhaps in a similarly conceived vegetable plot. A dark passageway of yew might be floored with pale gravel to reflect light, with a glimpse of white planting or sweeping lawns at the far end. A fruit tunnel, on the other hand, might be positioned to lead to an orchard or vegetable garden. Your own imagination is the best guide.

Freshly planted willow stems, even without their foliage in winter, can be used to create a fascinating pattern. The rhythm of the arching stems is echoed by the curve of the path that disappears with an air of mystery. Chipped bark provides a low-maintenance floor that perfectly complements the informal nature of the feature.

METAL ARBOURS

Where metal is of a sufficiently heavy gauge, rust can give it a warmth and patina that is rarely achieved by painting. This delightful fruit arbour provides a secret and shady retreat in which to relax on a hot summer's day.

Characteristics: Metal arbours are visually lighter than those built of timber, and if painted black are almost invisible from a distance. This gives them a great delicacy, in spite of their strength, and allows climbers virtually to float over the surface. There are fine old examples in many historic gardens, usually constructed from wrought iron, although the more brittle cast iron was sometimes employed in wonderful patterns. You can still obtain good wrought-iron arbours, but they are generally made to order by craftsmen blacksmiths, and are expensive. Arbours made from plastic-coated metal or bent wire are also available, but tend to lack visual strength, even when covered by climbers.

I have designed arbours using heavy gauge galvanized piping, bent to shape and painted in glorious primary colours. These look terrific, and can form a powerful focal point, especially when positioned against a dark background of planting.

Uses: Metal arbours are used in exactly the same way as those made from timber.

Construction: Virtually all metal arbours, apart from the very simplest designs that can be constructed from bent steel rods or thick wire, are made by craftsmen. Most designs have legs that are bent over at the bottom to form an anchor set in a concrete foundation.

Contrasting & associating materials: Metal arbours blend well into a wide range of settings, but remember always that it is important to respect the overall style of the garden.

Simplicity is all-important in a garden, and this delicious hoop frames the seat below and links the two clipped box balls on either side. The ivy smothering the pierced wall behind the bench has started to work its way over the arbour.

WOODEN ARBOURS

Timber is an infinitely flexible design material providing every opportunity to create something that is unique. Simple geometric shapes will be the most successful, and in this example the planting plays second fiddle to the structure itself.

Co-ordination within a composition is always important, and this seat has either been purpose-built or impeccably chosen to blend with the rhythmically arched roof above. Fragrant planting, such as jasmine or honeysuckle, would be a natural choice for such a seat.

Characteristics: An arbour is a static feature, usually sited at some distance from the house and main terrace, which should provide an important focal point in the overall design of the garden. It will entice you to it, give vertical definition to the space, and act as host to fragrant climbing plants. The style in which it is built should relate directly to the rest of the garden, and ideally it should be positioned to adjoin, or be surrounded by, planting, which will naturally soften its outline.

Timber is a beautifully flexible material and there is virtually no limit to the design possibilities for a wooden arbour. Just bear in mind that simple structures are usually more successful than complicated ones. A number of off-the-peg designs are available, but these are often small and of dubious value; you can usually do far better yourself. Arbours need to be big enough to incorporate a table and chairs (though benches can be built into the framework to save space). Diminutive examples may look pretty, but will have little practical value as a sitting area.

Uses: An arbour will provide an informal sitting area, a place for relaxation, a place to pause at the end of a path, or, tucked away, a place to be 'happened' on. You must be led to it, rather than through it.

Construction: Depending on its design, a wooden arbour will either be a straightforward carpentry job or a more complicated one. Hardwood, or pre-treated softwood can be used, and posts should be generous in their dimensions: at least 10cm (4in) square, and often more. They should be set in concrete foundations or adjustable shoes driven into the ground. The sides can be left open, or filled with one of the many designs of trellis available, which will provide support for climbers. The roof will be an open structure, and although timber can be used for this in a variety of ways, wrought iron will also make an excellent and delicate ceiling. The floor can be formed from one of a whole range of surfaces, from grass to brick paving, though hard materials provide a better all-weather surface.

Contrasting & associating materials: Arbours are adaptable, and should reflect the style and materials used in their immediate surroundings. Heavy, rustic timbers might be used in a woodland area, or crisply sawn and planed boards in a more contemporary situation. Floor paving should follow suit.

OVERHEAD BEAMS

Although overhead beams are the simplest of structures, they succeed immediately in defining the vertical space beneath them, providing an informal ceiling. Climbers, in this case wisteria, can be used to soften the line and cast a dappled shade beneath.

Characteristics: Overhead beams help to define the space beneath them, and by extending the line of a house or other building out into the garden or landscape, visually and physically help to tie the two elements together. Overheads are normally made of timber, and link best with a timber building; however, colour can also be used to reinforce it. They should be left as an open structure; any roofing, whether of clear plastic or any other material, will simply collect debris, and sound like thunder in any but the lightest shower. Overheads are found, in different vernacular forms, all over the world: from rough-hewn timbers on the Indian sub-continent to crisp sawn and planed boards on the west coast of America.

Uses: As well as the uses mentioned above, overheads can also break a view providing privacy from the upstairs windows of neighbouring properties; give dappled shade; and play host not only to a child's swing, but also to fragrant climbing plants or hanging containers for plants.

OVERHEAD BEAMS
Either run overhead beams out from the house or from a free-standing wall. Use 220 × 50mm (9 × 2in) timbers joists, set in hangers off the wall and supported by scaffolding poles at their extremities.

JOIST HANGER
Either build joist hangers into a new wall, or insert them into an existing one.

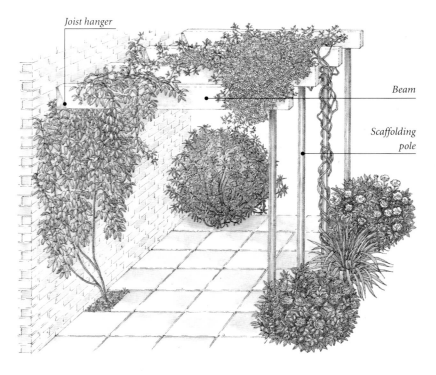

Joist hanger

Beam

Scaffolding pole

Construction: Timber can be worked in many ways, and overheads should be used to match the style of the adjoining architecture. As a general rule, the simpler the construction the better, and beams usually look best with square cut ends rather than being nosed off at an angle or cut into complicated patterns.

Beams are usually fitted to the house with joist hangers, and supported at the other end by a cross beam fixed to timber uprights or screwed to metal poles (which often look best painted black). Uprights should be firmly concreted into the ground, and timber should be pre-treated against rot, or painted. An ample depth of topsoil should be left around the uprights to accept climbing plants, and, depending on the planting, uprights and beams may need wires run through metal eyes so that climbers can be tied in.

Contrasting & associating materials: Overhead beams should associate with the architecture and garden they adjoin. Crisply sawn timbers will look perfect with geometric paving, bold railway sleepers and gravel. Rough-hewn beams will sit comfortably with more relaxed, natural and informal surfaces.

ATTACHING POLES TO BEAMS
Fit scaffolding poles with a timber dowel before using a double-ended screw to fix the latter into the beam.

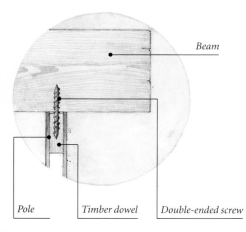

Beam

Pole *Timber dowel* *Double-ended screw*

AWNINGS

Characteristics: Awnings can be reeled out from fittings attached to the house, or simply draped over a framework of overhead beams and roughly fixed in position to prevent them blowing off in the wind. At their most basic, and mobile, they can be formed from a sheet thrown over a frame or the branches of a tree. Fabric can be water-proofed canvas or polyesters, both of which come in a wide range of colours, or woven matting, easily purchased from a store or local craftsperson. Plain colours are often the most successful, and in a sophisticated situation the colour or pattern of the awning and outside cushions can be chosen to echo the interior design of the house. Although white can be elegant, it may be rather glaring in strong sunlight and it also shows dirt easily. Thin muslin, though, will filter the sunlight, producing near magical conditions beneath its shade, and it can be tied into wonderful swagged tents to create a particular style or atmosphere. The disadvantage is that being such a fine fabric, it has a relatively short life.

Uses: The purpose of an awning is to cast shade, either to provide agreeable sitting conditions for people, or to prevent fabrics and furniture inside the house from bleaching in sunlight. They can also be used in a mobile and delightfully informal way to provide an enticing oasis of shade anywhere in the garden.

Construction: Awnings can be bought in kit form, complete within a boxed framework of variable size that can be bolted into position. Alternatively, fabric can be cut to size, finished off if there are raw edges, and casually slung over beams or a more informal structure in the garden.

Contrasting & associating materials: Awnings will have a natural affinity with other fabrics in the garden or in the adjoining house. They can also be used to match or contrast with the paintwork, paving, or even plants; a pale fabric, for example, would make an effective contrast with darker paintwork on the walls.

In this austere but superbly architectural situation the awning introduces beautifully contrasting elements of softness and delicacy. The use of finer fabrics for awnings tends to filter the sunlight slightly rather than blocking it out entirely, and can therefore look more effective and attractive than heavier materials would.

A garden without features of any kind is a clean canvas and to bring such a garden to life requires careful planning.

Even while working out the initial framework of boundaries, surfaces, trees and planted areas, you will be thinking about positioning major focal points strategically within the design.

Some items, such as sheds and greenhouses, will be functional, although they should still look good; others, such as water features, rock gardens or raised beds, will be decorative; while others still, such as swimming pools, provide a specific activity.

All major features, however, will play an important visual role drawing the eye and it is vital they are positioned carefully. There is an unlimited number of ways that a feature can be built or interpreted. But, precisely because it forms a focal point, it is important that it is in harmony with the garden, and that the feature is chosen and sited with care. To position an informal, irregularly shaped pool in a formal terrace would simply make it look incongruous, as would placing a traditional summerhouse in an *avant-garde* design.

In general terms, the key to choosing and using features is to remember that the areas closest to a building are naturally more architectural or formal than those farther away, where the design can become softer and looser. Whereas crisply designed seating, or rectangular raised beds will sit comfortably nearer the house, a winding stream or tree house will be more appropriate for the farther parts of the garden.

The position of some features will additionally be determined by their use. It makes sense to site a barbecue close to the kitchen, and a play area in view of the house. A rock garden or greenhouse will benefit from an open, sunny aspect, while a shed may well need screening. The position of others may be affected by climate; a swimming pool that is used all the year round in a warmer climate may be best sited near the house. In a temperate climate, where it is likely only to be used in summer, this might be better set in a sheltered position, further away from the house.

Certain features will also be suggested by the topography of the site. A sloping garden lends itself to water, in the form of streams, cascades and pools, with rockwork adding a further dimension. Flat gardens, on the other hand, are ideal for expansive pools that set up ever-changing reflections.

Of course, with any feature, there is a degree of on-going maintenance that must be considered early in the design process, whether this be

treating a timber building against decay or weeding a rock garden. Also, depending on your choice of feature, you or your contractor will need to check location regulations on siting and using a swimming pool, as well as soil conditions, water table, access to power, water and drainage.

As a final thought, do not assume that features are permanent: as children grow up a playhouse could be transformed into a romantic folly, a garden pool a bog garden. One of the greatest pleasures of a garden is that it grows and evolves and so can adapt to your changing lifestyle.

Opposite: An unusual water feature such as this one provides a strong focal point and should be carefully positioned. The angled cups allow the water to cascade down, while the background irises provide a delicate counterpoint.

Left: This focal point not only stands out in sharp relief against the background but also has a roof with a strong vertical emphasis that draws the eye upwards.

Above: Some places are special, and because of that become natural focal points. The crisp decking and chairs used in this design introduce a successful architectural element into an otherwise soft composition.

FORMAL PONDS

Classical formality usually relies on repetitive geometry which can be static, but the introduction of water introduces both movement and a delicate sound.

Characteristics: Formality in a garden is a powerful element, often producing a rigid and balanced framework that benefits from softening. This can be done in a number of ways: planting is an obvious choice, but water, with its changing moods, reflections and movement can be another perfect team player. Great gardens using water in a formal way are found throughout the world, from the majestic splendour of the great Italian Renaissance compositions, to the Moorish courts of the Alhambra. In hot climates water provides a cooling influence and reflections under wide skies, whereas in the softness of a temperate climate it gives a feeling of tranquillity. Even on a small scale a formal pool, if correctly conceived and sited, can introduce these same elements.

Formal pools look their best set within the geometry of a terrace close to a building, or within a balanced framework of lawns and hedges in the middle or more distant parts of the garden. Near the house, a pool will normally be designed into the hard landscape framework of a terrace, often in a rectangular shape as part of the overall paving pattern. In lawns and planted areas, pools may be edged with stone, set with statuary, and furnished with exquisite fountains. Here, the shape may be either rectangular or circular rather than curving freely, and this can be reflected in the planting of surrounding hedges or borders.

One of the most important uses of water is to introduce movement into an otherwise static design. The architect Sir Edwin Lutyens was a master of formality, and a genius with water, building superbly detailed pools, falls and chambers. By looking at his work you can start to understand the subtlety and importance of using such an element within a garden design. Although formality is often associated with traditional gardens, hi-tech and contemporary designs can use water in astonishing ways, contained within polished steel, fibreglass or sealed concrete shells.

Uses: Formal pools can be used both as a softening element within a strongly architectural area; as a focal point; or as a link between different parts of

A small water feature becomes more effective if it is raised closer to eye level. The brick coping, with its beautifully detailed corner, is at the perfect height here for sitting.

Formality is as pertinent in a contemporary setting as a traditional one. This composition of great strength and tranquillity proves that garden design can work as pure art.

the garden. Changes of level can provide opportunities for split-level pools, water cascades, or water staircases to link adjoining areas. If the water is moving, it will have an extraordinary influence in drawing you through the space – an effect that a row of fountains set down the length of a long pool will also have.

Construction: Many historic pools were built of stone set in watertight clay. Later, concrete replaced clay, but there were inevitable problems with settlement cracks and leakage. Today, different grades of butyl rubber, plastic and polyester laminates are used to form virtually indestructible liners.

Pools can be made shallow enough to form stairs or falls, or deep enough to support fish and planting. As a general rule, 600mm (2ft) is ample for domestic pools, and plants that enjoy shallow conditions can be positioned on marginal shelves. Levels must be carefully worked out and excavations given a smooth profile, with sharp stones removed and a base layer of damp sand laid to act as a cushion for the liner.

A simple formula for working out the size of liner you need, is to add twice the maximum depth to the maximum length and width of the pool. The liner is then positioned and loosely anchored around the edge of the pool with bricks or coping, and water is run in until the liner is moulded into shape. Once the water has nearly reached the top of the excavation, it can be trimmed to shape, nicked to make it lie flat around any curves, and the coping laid to overhang the water and create a line of shadow. With rectangular pools there is always a tendency for the liner to pucker in the corners. Certain manufacturers will 'tailor' the liner by welding the sides and bottom, so that it fits the excavation exactly. Coping round the pool should match materials used elsewhere in the garden, and if you are thinking of using statuary, it, too, must be chosen and positioned with great care to match the mood of the overall composition. Fountains look fine in a formal pool, and if moving water

is required, this will probably be powered by submersible pumps, and power will have to be laid to the pool to cater for this.

Contrasting & associating materials: Water is an adaptable element, and will blend into the widest possible range of settings and materials, both traditional and contemporary.

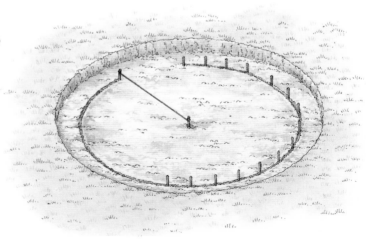

CONSTRUCTING A POND
Set out circular pools to a specific series of radii. Excavate the ground to a depth of 225mm (9in) for the marginal shelf, before digging to the full depth of 450mm (18in) being careful to angle the sides slightly. After removing any sharp stones, add a base layer of damp sand or geo-textile to act as a cushion under the liner.

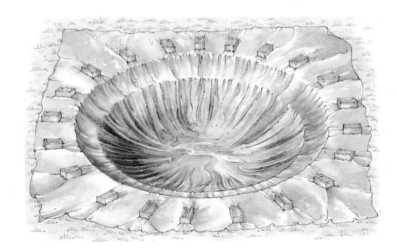

Once the excavation is complete, roughly place the liner into position and anchor it with bricks. When the water is run in, it will mould the liner to shape.

HARD EDGING FOR A LINER POND
Bricks set on edge in mortar just below the level of the surrounding turf form a crisp coping.

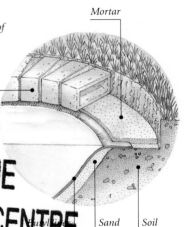

Mortar

Brick coping overhanging water

Sand   Soil

INFORMAL PONDS

Ideally, it should be impossible to tell that an informal pond has been artificially created. This is easier to achieve if the setting is large enough to handle a design of substantial size and conviction. A change of level also adds immeasurably to any such situation, providing the scheme with the bonuses of sound and movement.

Characteristics: While formal pools demand an architectural treatment, their informal counterparts, more fluid in shape, will blend into the farther parts of the garden, relating to lawns and borders with strong flowing curves, which in turn set up a real feeling of space and movement.

The larger the pool, the more generous associating features can be. A simple bench and sitting area will probably look just right by a small pool. However, on the banks of a large area of water that is verging on being a lake, a generous summerhouse, boathouse or other major feature would look in perfect scale.

Classical fountains and statuary are difficult to use successfully in an informal pool, but planting can provide a wonderful extra dimension, both in the water and surrounding the feature, blending it into the wider garden. Moisture-loving plants, with their bold foliage, are among the most handsome on the garden designer's palette. All water benefits from an open position that is not overhung by too many trees.

Uses: Informal pools are wonderfully versatile in their uses: they are a haven for wildlife of all kinds; they set up reflections that mirror the changing moods of the surrounding composition and the sky above; they act as major focal points at any time of the year. Any area of open water can be a hazard to young children, who should always be supervised when near it, but pools can provide hours of fascination and learning for youngsters. If you are lucky enough to have a lake, then the pleasures of boating and simply messing about on the water will be quite irresistible.

Construction: The curves of an informal pool should be laid out with great care. The disastrous technique, encouraged in so many gardening books, of casting a hosepipe on the ground, kicking it about, and then cutting out the shape, should be avoided at all costs; it simply produces a convoluted series of wiggles that are hard on the eye and a chore to maintain. Instead, observe how nature handles curves, particularly in a watery situation, and do the same: the shape will always be positive, generous and gentle. You can achieve this best by drawing the curves with a pair of compasses on the drawing board, sweeping one bold curve into the next, and then setting these out in the garden by swinging a line from the radii involved.

Like formal pools, the majority of informal pools are lined with butyl rubber or laminated plastic. In some situations, coping will be unnecessary: a grassy bank, poolside planting, cobble and boulder beach or boggy area could all be created to blend the water softly into its surroundings.

Contrasting & associating materials: Lawns, planting and beaches of various kinds are the perfect counterpoints to informal water. Coping stones or coping brick should almost certainly match materials used elsewhere in the garden. Decking looks superb, as do the more relaxed forms of paving such as random rectangular paving, granite setts and brick.

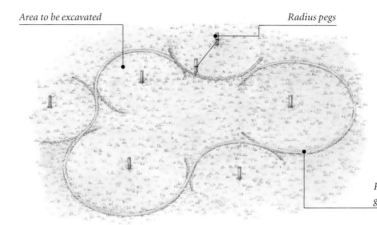

Area to be excavated   Radius pegs

MARKING OUT AN INFORMAL POOL

Radii can be of any size, but the more generous the better, with one curve running smoothly into the next. When designing a pool remember that a marginal shelf will be approximately 225mm (9in) wide and deep, which will reduce the area of deeper water.

Radiused curves scored on to grass or marked out with sand

MARGINAL PLANTING AT THE EDGE OF A POND

To form a bog garden, or damp area at the edge of a pond, allow water to seep into an adjoining bed that is contained by a continuation of the butyl liner.

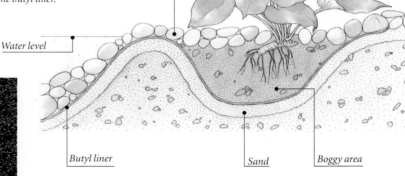

Loose pebble beach allowing seepage

Water level

Butyl liner   Sand   Boggy area

INFORMAL EDGING FOR A LINER POND

An informal 'beach' can be formed with loose cobbles set on a gently sloping shelf around the edge of the pond.

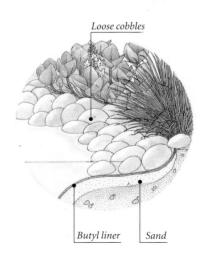

Loose cobbles

Butyl liner   Sand

This is a perfect and fascinating example of how an essentially formal pattern can be softened by planting. While the trickle of water introduces movement, the Pachysandra *overhanging the water transforms a simple composition into something more mysterious.*

WOODEN BRIDGES

There is a narrow line between the production of design for design's sake and the creation of a work of art. I place this bridge in the latter category, with its highly stylized pattern

and Japanese overtones, and its narrow approach that guides you strictly down a specific route. The planting provides the perfect counterpoint to this formal design.

can while away endless hours. Once again, the style of the bridge should suit the underlying design of the garden. Bridges are dramatic features in themselves, but the drama is often overdone, with bright red Japanese designs placed in quiet country gardens, or hideously overworked and garishly white structures in quite ordinary situations. Never be tempted into design for design's sake of this kind; forget the glossy manufacturers' catalogues with their horrendous prices; instead, look around you at vernacular styles, and remember back to the simple designs you saw as a child. Then get a skilled local craftsman to use his commonsense and knowledge to build you a bridge; the results should be more than worthwhile.

Uses: Bridges are quite simply paths across water and otherwise impassable areas, but they are also important directional tools. Water, even at its shallowest, is a real deterrent to access, and a

Characteristics: Timber is one of the most adaptable of materials, and can be considered for a variety of uses in the garden and to create virtually any style, shape or pattern. When it is used for bridges, the advantages are obvious: you can build structures from the simplest planks laid across a brook, to a complex structure that soars over a stream or inlet.

Bridges are one of the ultimate tension points, as they lead you across what is essentially an alien element at a specific point in the composition. This can set up all kinds of interesting possibilities, from the excitement of wobbling across logs or railway sleepers set over a boggy area, to the wistful enjoyment of leaning over the solid handrail of a sturdy bridge to enjoy the sight and sound of water sliding underneath.

Bridges are rarely devices to be hurried across, and the broader and more generous they are, the more pleasurable the experience. Children adore them, which is the best justification for sound construction and safety; the fun of playing 'Pooh sticks', or bombing leaves with anything to hand,

Is this the path to a secret garden over a small stream that is full of movement and trout for tickling? The bridge, built from two railway sleepers and bordered with sensibly sturdy

handrails, is impeccably simple and unsophisticated. The temptation to cross this bridge and walk down the flower-edged path beyond is almost irresistible.

METAL BRIDGES

well-sited bridge can open up a whole new area of garden – on an island, or the farther side of a stream. Apart from crossing water, there are other situations where a bridge might be used to span a lane or deep gully in a woodland area. On a smaller scale, even a simple structure over a garden pool can dramatically influence the way in which you move around the garden.

Construction: Bridges should be built to a scale appropriate for the use they can expect: whether for pedestrians, animals, vehicles, or perhaps all three. Their use and situation will often determine the final shape and therefore the skills, and the expense, involved. A large span over deep water or across a rocky gully may well need to be arched for strength, fitted with robust handrails for safety, and bolted down to secure concrete foundations on either side; this is an advance joinery project that will probably require help from a professional. A bridge forming a mere continuation of a track over a rill might simply consist of logs cut to length, roughly shaped, and secretly bedded on either bank. Between these two extremes lies a wealth of sensible design that can be carried out by most competent carpenters. Many bridge projects use similar techniques to decking, and the latter can often be adapted or extended to cross water in the most imaginative ways.

Hardwood handrails are usually more handsome, and certainly more durable, than softwood rails, and they can be worked in a variety of fascinating patterns. Any timber, hard or soft, will need initially and regularly thereafter to be treated to withstand rot.

Contrasting & associating materials: This will depend on the situation (timber bridges could be an extension of a timber deck, a gentle continuation of an informal path through a woodland, or a crisp contrast to pale pre-cast paving), but the right or wrong design decision can make or mar a composition. In other words, use your head and do not get seduced by pictures in glossy magazines.

Metal can be both incredibly strong and visually light, and it can be used to span greater distances than would be possible using timber. This delicate tracery, with its braced handrails, allows the view to run through the bridge, and the sweeping line introduces a feeling of movement. The whole construction has been painted in black, the ideal colour.

Characteristics: Metal has a strength and delicacy that sets it apart from other materials. These characteristics make it suitable for large spans which can float over water, and for a wide range of styles, both traditional and contemporary. Metal is often used as a substructure for timber, with the metal providing strength for the main frame, and timber being used for the walkway and rails.

You can see fine examples of cast-iron bridges in many historical gardens, and since the full potential of the material took some time to be realized, the earliest sometimes have wood-working joints. The most sophisticated bridges, used in grand gardens with other major features, are suspension bridges, where delicacy of design is combined with great strength.

Contemporary bridges are usually built from a variety of steel, wire and mesh, and as most metal, apart from stainless steel, is painted, this allows a link to be made with colours used elsewhere in the garden. As a general landscape colour, however, black is hard to beat, and will blend into virtually any background; white is far too visually demanding, and should be used with extreme circumspection.

Uses: As metal is immensely strong, these bridges can be used to span distances where timber or stone would fail, and to cater for even the heaviest vehicles. However, metal can also be used to construct the most exquisite and charming small pedestrian bridges.

Construction: Metal is a specialist material, and bridges are almost invariably designed by experts and fabricated off-site, before being assembled in the garden.

Contrasting & associating material: The materials used for the bridge should match those of the surrounding landscape. A steel bridge will perfectly complement a building of steel and glass, while a subtly arched wrought- or cast-iron structure could soar between lawns or woodland. Surrounding hard landscape materials should follow the same philosophy.

STONE BRIDGES

The simplest of bridges can be formed using roughly hewn slabs of natural stone; once positioned, these will remain permanently in position. The staggered pattern shown here provides an interesting variation on a straight crossing.

Characteristics: As with a timber bridge, the style of a stone bridge can be simple or complicated: from a straightforward slab laid over a garden pool or brook, to the full-blown splendour of a Palladian masterpiece spanning a lake. The differences are obvious, both in situation and cost. Stone is not only more expensive, but both visually and physically harder than timber. As with any structure, the type and colour of stone used, and the building style, needs to blend into the overall setting.

Uses: Stone is one of the strongest and most durable materials you can use in the garden. It is also the heaviest, and so its first resting place will almost certainly be its last. In other words, you need to get it sited right first time! Stone bridges are suitable for all kinds of access, but particularly where the bridge is to carry heavy loads and support heavy wear.

Construction: This will again depend on the complexity of the project. A sizeable slab of stone can be manhandled into position with the help of many bodies and basic tools. It will probably not need foundations or shaping in any way. A full-blown arch, on the other hand, will need comprehensive footings and a degree of skilled labour.

Contrasting & associating materials: Stone is very much a generic material, and looks best when it is used across the garden, not in isolation. A similar stone should be used throughout, and the style should echo the overall tone of the background composition. When mellowed, stone has the ability to complement nearly everything around it: paving, planting, lawns, water and woodland.

CONSTRUCTING STEPPING STONES ACROSS A POND

To ensure that the stepping stones are stable, build the piers on a foundation of 75mm (3in) smoothly trowelled concrete over a 150mm (6in) layer of hardcore. Set the slabs to just above water level, overlapping the piers.

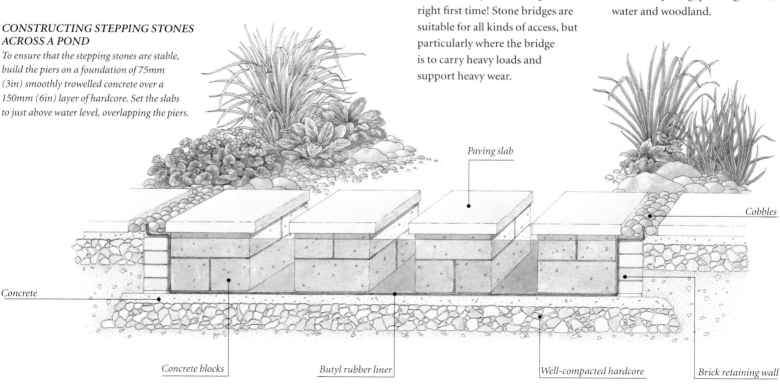

Paving slab

Cobbles

Concrete

Concrete blocks

Butyl rubber liner

Well-compacted hardcore

Brick retaining wall

Stepping stones make the ideal crossing for a small pool and can easily be set on piers made from concrete blocks or bricks. As a sensible precaution, use textured slabs to provide a good grip; these should be constructed to overhang the supporting piers by about 50mm (2in). The piers themselvs may be camouflaged by being painted black.

SMALL WATER FEATURES

Even the smallest pool can introduce both a cooling influence and a feeling of movement. The paving is an extraordinary, but successful, combination of concrete and broken plates, which contrasts effectively with the vibrant colours of the adjacent planting.

Characteristics: There are situations in which it may not be possible or desirable to have a large or even moderately sized pool: the garden may be tiny; shade may be a problem; a wide expanse of water could be a hazard to young children. There are, however, a range of features that are both safe for children, and can be tailored to fit even the smallest areas. Some, such as a millstone or boulder fountain, rely on re-circulated water being pumped up and over the surface from a sump concealed beneath. Others consist of a bowl or series of bowls that are fitted to a wall, with water spilling from one to the next, and eventually dropping to a small raised pool.

A superb contemporary feature known as a Kügel consists of a polished sphere of granite that floats on low-pressure jets of water just clear of a matching cup, also made of granite. The feature is fitted with solenoids that control the water jets, turning the ball slowly one way and then another, allowing sunlight to sparkle off the surface. It is perfectly safe and irresistible to even the smallest children, whose tiny fingers cannot be trapped beneath the revolving surface.

Water will help to cool an area on the hottest summer's day, but it is the sight and sound of water that is the most important reason for finding a place for it in a garden. Water is one of the most valuable elements in helping to relieve stress, and watching an ever-changing cascade or a bubble-jet fountain can evoke an extraordinary feeling of peace.

Uses: Small features can, of course, be used where space is at a premium, but can also provide a point of emphasis in many parts of the garden. Because of their intimate scale, they often look best and feel

WATER FEATURE WITH BOULDERS

To create this feature, set a large water tank in level ground. Build piers inside the tank to support the boulders, filling the spaces around them with smaller smooth stones. Position a submersible pump in the base of the tank to send water in two directions: straight up through a drilled boulder, and out of the tank and through another drilled boulder to spray water back into the tank below. Use valves to control the flow.

There are endless variations on this theme where water can be pumped over and through drilled rocks or millstones.

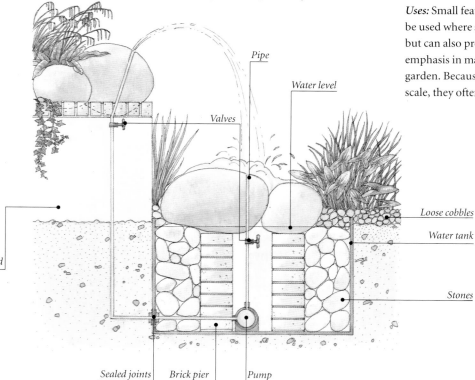

Pipe

Water level

Valves

Loose cobbles

Water tank

Stones

Raised bed

Sealed joints   Brick pier   Pump

Good humour is an essential part of successful garden design, and while this is a highly individualistic statement, it is also successful. The contrast of materials and colours is particularly telling, and the sound effects must be delightful.

most comfortable set within or close by a sitting area, and are often most telling when positioned so that they can be seen from within the house. Apart from their obvious visual and audible qualities, they will also provide a valuable source of water for birds, butterflies and bees.

Construction: Almost all these features use re-circulated water fed from a submersible pump. The millstone, or its derivative, is usually set on piers built up within a tank and level with its top, while the pump is placed on the bottom, and the area between the top of the tank and the stone is covered with a metal mesh, concealed by loose cobbles and boulders, before the tank is then filled with water. A simple dipstick will tell you when to top the feature

up; it is surprising how much evaporation can take place on a hot summer's day.

Wall plaques, bowls and similar water features are usually set into the surface of the wall and held in position with metal ties, along with any associated plumbing.

Contrasting & associating materials: All these features are highly individualistic and should be chosen carefully to suit their surroundings. A series of cast stone wall cascades might be appropriate for a formal area or chic town garden, whereas a large boulder, drilled through the middle and spilling water on to a bed of cobbles would suit a less formal situation. A contemporary Kügel would fit best in a modern setting, whereas a millstone would look

The symbolism of Japanese gardens is both delicate and difficult to reproduce as each component has its own special significance. However, when handled correctly, the results can be stunning, with a great sense of permanence and stability.

FOUNTAINS

There is a great deal of drama and movement in this design, both in the fountain that breaks the surface of the spa bath, and in the soaring steps that burst right through the wall

and lead into the garden beyond. The details shown here are next to a swimming pool, resulting in a composition that is entirely complementary.

Characteristics: Fountains have been around for centuries, and many of the oldest classical gardens used them in abundance. You have only to visit the great Renaissance gardens of Italy to see fountains in all their magnificent glory, drama and raw power. The secret of their success lies in their relationship to the surrounding garden, and this all depends on scale. Whereas a large garden can accommodate a sizeable pool complete with a correspondingly large fountain, problems arise in small gardens when people insist on a soaring jet that both looks ostentatious and can quickly drain the pool dry – the slightest breeze will blow the water out of the area.

In a formal situation, a fountain can make the most telling focal point at the end of a vista, and fountains arching in from the sides, or set in line down the middle, will lead the eye down the length of a long stretch of water. In an asymmetric design, a fountain can be offset, to balance another feature in a different part of the garden. The height and shape of a fountain can also differ dramatically: while a single, simple plume has ultimate elegance, there is rugged power in a gushing jet, and tranquillity in a bubble just

breaking the surface of a large, flat pool. There are innumerable different designs of fountain, and ways in which they can be used, but as with all garden design, the simpler statements work best.

The background to a fountain should always be carefully considered. A fountain seen against a pale sky will become almost invisible; if viewed against a darker plane of hedging or planting, the plume will be thrown into sharp relief.

Uses: The prime use of a fountain is to draw the eye and form a focal point, whether this be dramatic or low-key. A secondary function, and one that can be vital in a fish pond, is to aerate the water in the pool. In addition to this, there is no doubt that a water jet has a cooling influence, both real and psychological.

Construction: The height and volume of water in a fountain will depend on the size of pump driving it. Today, virtually all pumps are submersible, safe, relatively cheap to run, and have a long life. A valve is often incorporated between the pump and the jet, and this can be used to control the volume of water reaching the head.

Different fountain heads create different effects, from a single narrow plume to a widely dispersed ring of separate jets. A jet can also be set beneath the water, when it will create a bubble or simply ripple the surface.

Pumps today are completely sealed and therefore very safe, but it should be remembered that electricity is a potential killer in a garden, particularly in the proximity of water. Correct wiring, run through a conduit, is essential, as is a circuit-breaker connected into its own separate socket. If in doubt, it is *always* wise to employ a qualified electrician.

Contrasting & associating materials: Fountains are essentially self-contained, and although usually set in a pool, they can issue from a boulder or other feature. They should take their cue from the composition of the overall design. I have recently designed a number of highly reflective acrylic pyramids which have bubble fountains issuing from slots in the surface, creating the most stunning effects in sunlight. Do not be shy; the possibilities are endless.

Not only are fountains effective used as focal points, but they can also serve to divide a space or pierce a vista, encouraging you to pause before moving on.

STREAMS

By placing a few simple stones across this stream the designer has succeeded in creating a bridge that doubles as a weir. This has the effect of backing the water up, allowing it to cascade over the feature as a small waterfall. This creates both movement and sound, two vital ingredients in a large-scale composition of this kind.

Characteristics: Streams are, by definition, natural features, and it is not easy to reproduce this effect. The manner in which a contrived stream flows through the garden will inevitably make it a major design element, and you will have to decide where it will start or finish, whether you need to cross it, whether you want to plant the margins, and how it will relate to the garden around it. Before you begin, go and look at examples of the real thing; sketch, take photographs, and get a feel for creation.

Streams can be short or long, narrow and rushing, or wide and slow, depending on where you build them and the effect you want to achieve. They can be used within a rock garden, around outcrops from the bottom of a fall, or flowing gently through rolling lawns to enter a pool at a lower level, or, indeed, to encompass all of these.

A slope is obviously a prerequisite, and the nature of this slope will naturally affect the speed of water over the ground. A fast flow over rocks and steeply falling ground will be more dynamic and attention-seeking than a meandering affair working its way down a shallow gradient.

If you are lucky enough to possess a natural stream, it can often be modified to make it even better. Modifications might include a diversion, with sections dammed to form pools, weirs and falls, and meanders created that could link in with the flowing lines of lawns and borders.

Uses: All moving water has strong directional emphasis, and will lead both feet and eye through a garden. A stream can bind together various parts of the composition: it might issue from planting or a small spinney, tumble down rocks that lead to a pool, exit at the other side, flow through a boggy area, pass under a bridge, bend past a sitting area and summerhouse, and empty into a large holding pool at the bottom of the slope. It can also divide the garden, perhaps separating a controlled, formal design from a far less formal area given over to rougher grass, trees and indigenous planting.

Construction: The bed of a natural stream will be basically watertight, but if you change its direction this may not be the case. (If you tamper with a natural watercourse you may also need to let your local Water Authority know.) In this situation, the new course will need lining with a naturally impermeable material, such as clay; a job for a specialist landscape contractor.

If you are creating a new stream, avoid using concrete on its own, which tends to crack imperceptibly over a period of time, and use butyl or laminated plastic liners bedded on a cushioning layer of wet concrete. Cover the liner with more concrete, which protects the surface and allows stones to be loosely tumbled in to form a natural bed. You can spend hours painstakingly positioning rocks and stones, but it is not worth it; nature bundles them down the banks and over the bottom in a totally random pattern, and that is the technique you should adopt too.

The size of the pool at the end of the circuit is of major importance. This will play host to a submersible pump that will draw water from the bottom pool, pump it to the top of the run, and fill the stream on the way back to the bottom. When the pump is switched on, the level of water in the lower or feeder pool will drop (more or less, according to the length of the run and the volume of water required). Unless this pool is sufficiently large, you will always need to top up the water level because you are draining water from this pool to fill the rest of the circuit. Do this either with a hosepipe, or, in sophisticated systems, with an automatic float switch. A feeder pool with only twice the volume of the rest of the circuit will therefore lose half of its water. When you switch the pump off, the water will flow back from the stream and cause the pool to overflow, so it is worth installing an outfall pipe to prevent this from happening.

Contrasting & associating materials: Streams associate with all those materials found in a natural setting: rock, planting, grass and trees. Build bridges to fit into their surroundings; construct paving for any adjoining sitting areas from natural materials; and be sure that the design of any adjacent building is sympathetic.

WATERFALLS

Characteristics: If you are lucky enough to live in an upland area, and part of your garden contains a natural stream and waterfall, you will know just how beautiful this feature is. 'Fallingwater', one of Frank Lloyd Wright's most dynamic houses, was set amid a series of falls, with water sliding and sweeping around the architecture. Few of us have the opportunity to match this, but the drama of falling water is a powerful one.

Natural falls, both real and created, have a gloriously informal character, but it is perfectly possible to create a dramatic, closely controlled formal waterfall within a supremely architectural framework. This might take the form of a classical cascade issuing from a high terrace or falling on either side of steps (both of which have considerable historical precedent), or a sharply detailed leading edge design that uses polished steel, glass and concrete to form a series of water chutes and falls. The great American contemporary landscape architect Lawrence Halprin designs massive and wonderful cascades in sharply modelled and board-finished concrete. These interpret the streams and falls of his beloved high sierra, but in a style that is timeless.

Unfortunately, such imitations all too often fail to live up to the real thing, and at worst are downright degrading. Scale is all-important here: the usual fault is

a lack of boldness, where the feature is reduced to insignificance. Just occasionally, the pendulum swings the other way, and boldness becomes gross and overblown; there is not much to choose between the two. The most common fault is to build a large feature and then have an under-powered pump that results in a feeble fall. If you build big, then power generously; if the fall is small (which is often equally, if not more, effective), you should still use a generous pump.

You can easily valve it down to the flow you want, but it is impossible to do the opposite.

Uses: Waterfalls are great linking elements, leading the eye down a slope, or a dramatic change of level. They can reinforce the line of a path or steps, create enormous movement, and act as major focal points. One of their great attributes is the sound of tumbling water, and large falls can even be used to combat background noise, such

CONSTRUCTING A WATERFALL
A submersible pump circulates the water from the feeder pool to the top pool.

Water level

Stone to form fall

Butyl liner

Liners bonded with mastic and sandwiched between stones

Sand   Feeder pool

CREATING A NATURAL SETTING
Always build falls to look as natural as possible, bearing in mind that the lower or feeder pool should always have a considerably greater volume than the higher pool. Be sure to keep any surrounding rocks and planting in scale with the overall feature.

The Japanese influence is strong here, as demonstrated by the depth of understanding apparent in the dynamics of how the water has been used and the way in which the surrounding rocks have been set to maximum effect. The whole scene is strongly sculptural, the vertical stones serving to emphasize and enhance the line of the fall.

as that of traffic. In Halprin's Freeway Park in Seattle, the huge waterfalls completely drown the noise of an eight-lane highway that passes underneath !

Construction: All waterfalls take skill to set and build properly. If you are thinking of tackling the job yourself, go and see how nature has done it – almost invariably, pretty well!

For a natural design, stone will need to be set at a specific angle, or bedding plane, to match any surrounding outcrops; the lip will need to be angled to shed water in the pattern you want; and ancillary rocks, such as fall stones, should be positioned under the flow to throw the water away from the face. After many years of experience, I have found that butyl liners are the best for keeping pools and falls watertight, but it is important to set the rocks and cover the pool floor in concrete; this both hides and protects the liner, and makes it easier to bed the various stones. The essential thing is to prevent water running back behind the liners, and out of the pool.

Contemporary falls often use a lip of glass, slate or marble to give a clean, crisp cascade, and these usually need a drip channel cut into the underside to prevent water running back under the sill. I am now using half-sections of black-painted guttering as a lip (in a variety of metals), set with the rounded side uppermost. The water spills off this perfectly cleanly, and it is both cheap and simple to install. Fibreglass and plastic pre-formed waterfalls are available in garden centres, but they are, on the whole, inferior and should definitely be avoided.

Contrasting & associating materials: These will depend entirely on the character of the feature, which will, in turn, reflect the character of the garden. Informal falls blend beautifully into well-built rock gardens in a relaxed part of the garden; crisp, contemporary falls look good with similar materials; and in a formal, possibly classical garden, sawn natural stone, gravel and wide lawns will complement the picture.

FORMAL SWIMMING POOLS

To an architectural designer, this composition would surely be pure heaven! There is line, form, a subtly reflective background and, above all, simplicity. Following the principle that form follows function, this pool not only looks stunning, but will also be a joy to swim in. The design certainly fulfils the maxim that less is more.

Characteristics: Open-air swimming pools can either be sited close to the house, where they become part of the hard landscaping that surrounds the building, or farther away, when they can be completely screened. Both are acceptable in design terms, and the choice will be influenced by the amount of use the pool gets, and the climate in which you live. Around the Mediterranean and in California, where the summers are long and the winters mild, a pool can be used for virtually the whole year, and as part of everyday life, it is probably best sited near the house. In more temperate climates the pool's use is inevitably more limited, and as the sight of an empty shell, or a sheet of freezing water, can be extremely depressing on a cold winter's day, you will do better to site the pool some distance away.

The use of classical columns, balustrade and Grecian statues smack more of an excavated Roman villa than a twentieth-century garden, and almost always looks ostentatious, but most formal pools have a strong architectural link of some kind with the area around them, which should naturally include changing rooms, the pool plant, and associated hard landscaping. Indoor pools are usually built as an integral part of the house, or as an extension to it, perhaps in a nearby barn or similar outbuilding.

Formal pools, whether indoor or out, are usually rectangular (the best shape for serious swimmers), sometimes with rounded ends, but are occasionally circular. You also need to think hard and long about the finish you want for the sides and bottom of the pool. Blue mosaic tiles are without doubt the most dull and overworked finish devised by man. Use mosaic by all means, but be aware that the designs need to be really well executed, in bold shapes and patterns, to avoid a fussy result. My taste tends to be rather purist and a single strong colour is generally enough for me: what about using deep red, green, or even black? Black is gloriously elegant as it tends to conceal the depth of the pool, though it has to be said that swimming in a black pool can be pretty creepy – like courting disaster from the creature of the black lagoon! David Hockney paints the walls of pools, and you could do the same; in fact, you can do nearly anything that appeals to you, so think about it.

As a final consideration, remember that any formal pool will be a dominant feature, and if it becomes the central focus of the overall composition, then the rest of the garden may have to radiate from it. If this is the effect you want, then that is fine, but it may be a good reason for

This composition is a glorious riot which simply hums with vibrancy and colour. Admittedly, the climate is sub-tropical or Mediterranean, which shows the strong colours to their best advantage, but it is a pity that few designers work in such a confident way. Although the pool is small, it is fitted with a powerful jet, allowing you to swim against the tide.

planning this as a self-contained area, screened by planting, contouring or some form of trellising. The need for shelter may be an additional reason: in a temperate climate, protection from walls, hedges or fences may dictate an entirely separate garden in its own right.

Uses: Apart from its obvious use, a swimming pool will be a major focus of life in the garden, and will provide a space devoted to sitting, dining, entertaining, barbecuing, and a good few other things besides. An intelligent design will incorporate all these, and wrap the area in planting. Linkage is important if the pool is set away from the house, and you will need to think about pathways, pergolas and other such features.

Construction: There are a number of different ways of building a pool, but despite what the kit manufacturers say, unless you are a builder this is a skilled job best left to the professionals.

Constructional materials for below-ground pools include concrete blocks, sprayed with additional concrete; pure-sprayed concrete shells with suitable reinforcing; and liners of various types that are fitted into a framework. You will also find above-ground pools, normally fabricated from liners within some kind of timber or metal frame. While these are relatively cheap and easy to erect, they often look pretty terrible and cause havoc if they are punctured!

The siting of plant and machinery, as well as changing facilities, will also have to be considered.

Contrasting & associating materials: A formal pool will sit comfortably in a formal situation. If the setting is traditional, then all the traditional materials, such as natural stone, brick and similar surfaces, will be suitable. If, however, you have a contemporary composition, then decking, pre-cast paving, plastics and imitation turf can all come into play. Many people view the latter with horror, but if you look upon it as waterproof carpet, and choose colours other than green, then all will be well.

You will certainly need a large budget, not to mention a spectacular setting, for a design on this scale! This superb pool, with its hint of classicism, provides a perfect example of understatement in design. The dramatic change of level gives the impression that the water is sliding off the edge of the hill and into the landscape beyond.

INFORMAL SWIMMING POOLS

Informality in design, with its sweeping shapes and dynamic forms, often brings with it a sense of space and movement. The secret of success here lies in the simplicity of line and the choice of materials which blend into the surrounding landscape. Enormous environmental responsibility is involved in dealing with a situation of this kind.

Characteristics: Here the scope is infinite, and virtually any shape can be used in an asymmetric or informal setting. Having said that, there is always a temptation to ignore the basic rules of simplicity or control: the ubiquitous kidney shape is probably the weakest and least satisfactory design shape ever conceived. Rectangles can also be used in an informal situation, and can often be mixed with curves to build up elegant shapes.

Americans, thanks in the main to their benign climate, are past masters at designing and building swimming pools. If you are thinking of building a pool, consult as many American books as you can, and notice how the finished pools are not only beautiful shapes, but are linked to their immediate and wider setting.

The hard landscape materials adjoining a free-form pool might, for example, be brushed aggregate concrete, or another fluid surface, such as industrial plastic flooring, or decking, which can be cut to shape. And in order to link the pool into the wider garden and the landscape beyond,

spoil from the excavation could form the basis for subtle and gentle contours, reinforced by planting and approached by sweeping paths. These shapes could be repeated in the surrounding lawns and borders, and the whole design could take its cue from the rolling countryside beyond.

Once again, the pool floor is important – while sweeping mosaic patterns in contrasting colours can be dramatic and link with the pool shape, a single colour often works best.

Uses: Much the same as for formal pools, except that the whole composition will be rather more laid back and relaxed.

Construction: If you are designing your own pool, the best way of creating satisfactory curves is to draw them out with a pair of compasses, sweeping one curve into the next in a naturally flowing pattern, before transferring the final design to the chosen site. Concrete sprayed over a reinforced frame is one of the most popular methods of

constructing free-form pools, as it will easily conform to any shape. As with formal pools, construction is really a job for the expert.

Contrasting & associating materials: Free-form pools call for fluid materials around them, or ones that can be easily cut to shape, such as decking. Let your imagination rip; you could create stunning effects with large boulders set within the surrounding paving, or a waterfall cascading into the deep end. The sensation of swimming under falling water is unsurpassed, and kids love it. You could have pool accessories, such as gushing jets, slides, diving boards to mention a few. Sculpture could be specially commissioned to pick up the shape or character of the pool; if it can also be swum through, or under, so much the better! But always try and choose everything to blend with the overall design, rather than tacking on extra details as afterthoughts. Design is about a creating a total environment, not just dislocated parts of it.

To me this has to be the ultimate swimming pool, although a degree of courage would be needed to swim in it! To produce such an effect, the change of level at the far side need not be very great, but should be just enough to break the sight line and create the sensation that you are swimming along the edges of the world.

ROCK FEATURES

Traditional rock gardens tend to be relatively labour-intensive features as they require regular attention if weeds are not to swamp the other plants. The stones used here,

which have acquired a rich and handsome patina of lichen, are of an ample size, and they have been set to a bedding plane that works its way down the slope.

Characteristics: Rock gardens, rock outcrops and rock features are all members of a family that has been much abused. At their best, they mirror nature in the closer confines of the garden, and act as wonderful hosts for a wide selection of specialist planting. At worst, the currant-bun rockery is a travesty of the real thing, often built from discarded lumps of concrete, and with more weeds than intended planting.

A true rockery will draw its inspiration from an upland landscape where rock outcrops naturally, and this is where you should go to get a feel of how to choose and set rock properly.

Different rocks have different characteristics: some are smooth, some deeply fissured, some split down their grain, while colours range from the speckled granites to dark red sandstones and pale limestones. The primary rule is to try to use a local stone, which is in plentiful supply. Fine stone found only in one region, which is probably also in limited supply, will never look completely at home anywhere else, and the cost of transporting it may well be exorbitant.

As an alternative to natural stone, there are a number of excellent imitation stones available. These are made from resins, fibreglass and crushed stone, and at their best they can be indistinguishable from the real thing.

Uses: Rock gardens, outcrops or just large boulders are focal points of differing intensity, but all provide vertical emphasis which demands attention. They can be used either as a vehicle for planting alpines and other specialist material, or left unplanted, as an outcrop in a grassed area, in woodland, or even in a paved area, where one or more large boulders can double as seats. A raised area such as this can also act as a screen or pivot, concealing another part of the garden and providing a feeling of mystery as a path winds into the space to reveal a secondary view.

Construction: The secret of using rock effectively lies in understanding how it outcrops naturally. When you see it in the landscape, all you will see is the top surface; the rest, like an iceberg, is concealed beneath the ground. This immediately presents a problem, for since the material is relatively expensive you will want to get visual value for your money, yet if you simply perch rocks on the surface the result will always look artificial. This may be valid as sculpture, but it will never look natural.

You will also see that rock in the landscape outcrops in lines, following the strata below the surface, and at a set angle, known as the bedding plane. A rock garden should also be set out in this way. Start by choosing a single stone, and set this in position to give you the line and the angle for the rest of the rocks. This keystone should, like all the other stones, be sunk into the ground to at least half its depth. One or two outlying rocks can be used to link the feature into the wider garden, and these, too, should follow the imaginary line of strata to give an impression of an extensive network beneath the garden.

The vast majority of alpine plants enjoy a gritty, free-draining soil, and it is important never to use subsoil when building a rock garden. Scree (fragments of rock broken down by natural weathering) can be used to form a top surface that will provide excellent drainage, and through which plants can grow. Rock gardens often look at their best in an informal part of the garden, but natural-looking outcrops can add high drama around a house or swimming pool.

Contrasting & associating materials: Rock looks its best alongside other natural materials from the same family. It would be a mistake to mix slate rockery stone with Cotswold or golden stone walling and York or grey stone paving; but in the west of England you will see slate paving, walling and rock looking superb together, with each element playing its individual role.

The Japanese have an innate understanding of rock and how it can be positioned to greatest effect in the garden. Using rock in such arrangements underlines the affinity of Japanese gardens with the wider landscape. In this highly stylized composition, the clipped shrub echoes and enhances the shape of the stone.

CONSTRUCTING A ROCK FEATURE
Set the rocks carefully at a similar angle or bedding plane to simulate a natural outcrop.

SUMMERHOUSES

This delightful display is the epitome of a traditional English country garden, with its sprawling roses, fragrant honeysuckle and the most inviting of garden buildings tucked away behind abundant flowers.

Small buildings with shady interiors are always irresistibly enticing, all the more so when they are tempered with planting and set below such an elegant roof.

Characteristics: It has come to pass that any old garden building, from a shed to a chalet, is now called a summerhouse – particularly by manufacturers keen to market their products.

Traditionally, a summerhouse was just that: a small building, built from local materials in a wide range of vernacular styles, usually set at some distance from the main house, to provide a hub for summer sitting, eating, entertaining and, first and foremost, the grand old habit of afternoon tea in the garden. Typically a product of a temperate climate, a summerhouse was designed to provide shelter from showers and wind, as well as from hot summer sun. Some houses can be turned round on a pivot to chase the sun, but this can position it at odds with sight lines and the rest of the garden alignment.

Uses: As a major focal point and as a centre of summer inactivity. Afternoon tea may have diminished in importance, but as a sitting place, surrounded by a terrace, the summerhouse can

play an important role in any overall garden design. It does, however, suggest that you have time to sit and relax. If you do, then this is the building for you. The temptation will be to use a summerhouse as a storeroom for general garden junk. Do not do this! If you need a shed, get one.

Construction: Stone, brick and timber are all suitable construction materials, with timber being the cheapest and most easily worked, and therefore the most common. Construction techniques will be the same as for any small building; your summerhouse will require sound foundations, flooring, walls and a roof. Some buildings are available in kit form, but these are often visually and physically flimsy.

Contrasting & associated materials: Materials used for the summerhouse should blend with those of the house or surroundings, though timber will feel comfortable in most settings. The same link can be made with adjoining paving.

GAZEBOS

This really is a room with a view, which is what gazebos are all about. Both the airy structure and the simple furniture are perfectly in harmony, and I particularly like the climber trained over the roof, which is bursting with character.

Characteristics: These are, correctly, garden buildings that are specifically set to embrace a view. In reality, the name has been adopted by many gardeners and manufacturers to mean anything from a shed to a summerhouse, however crude, which can be plonked down virtually anywhere.

Gazebos come in many different styles. They were originally landscape features, when good views were more prevalent, and would, and still should, reflect the style and the mood of the composition around them. They can be modern or traditional, small or large, but in the final analysis the view is the most important thing.

Uses: While some gazebos are set on top of a hill or at the end of a vista, I feel that they are at their most effective when tucked away wrapped in a degree of secrecy that makes them essentially informal and all the more attractive. Such places should be happened upon, rather than seeming to seek visual attention.

Construction: Like other garden buildings, they will be constructed from the widest range of materials: brick, stone, timber, metal, or a mixture of any of these. Very few are available for sale; the best will be built by craftsmen on site.

Contrasting & associating materials: Gazebos should be low-key and informal; their surroundings too. Floors can be old paving, brick, chipped bark, or simply beaten soil. Planting is a perfect foil, to blend the structure into its surroundings.

Some gazebos can be highly stylized, and while this is permissible, it means that such a feature must be sited with care if it is to be prevented from clashing with the surrounding garden. The gravel path here picks up on the white columns of the building.

SHEDS

Well-constructed plain wooden sheds have a certain no-nonsense elegance. Once it has weathered, a timber structure will blend into virtually any setting; this shed is softened by the random planting which surrounds it and the grand tree growing behind.

This beautifully built stone shed will last almost indefinitely; it is solid enough to act as a house, and many would welcome it as such! The plaque set over the door makes an attractive extra detail.

Characteristics: Every garden needs at least one shed. They are the utility workhorses of the wider composition and can serve a multitude of purposes. By their nature they are usually mundane structures, and it makes sense to screen them or tuck them away in an unobtrusive position. Access by a sound, wide path is important, as is some kind of adjoining hardstanding on which to park wheelbarrows and tools, or for use as an outdoor work space.

Most sheds can be bought prefabricated, and, as a general rule, it is worth going for the best-quality shed you can afford; it will pay dividends in length of service. It is also worth buying a size larger than you think you will need; sheds will always fill up faster than you expect. Styles vary enormously, and are available with double- or single-pitched roofs, and with doors and windows in different positions. Lean-to sheds that fit neatly against an existing wall can also be useful .

Uses: For storing tools, equipment, furniture, and anything else you can think of. Ideal as a workshop, for housing specialist equipment such as a filtration plant for a swimming pool, or, suitably modified, for animals of various kinds.

Construction: Although usually bought in kit form, and assembled on site, it is quite possible to build your own shed. Straightforward carpentry skills are needed, and the great advantage is that you can create the size and style you want. The shed will need a sound foundation: a concrete slab cast over a consolidated hardcore base is ideal, and paving slabs bedded in mortar over a similar base are also acceptable, though often unnecessarily expensive.

Woodwork will need regular applications of non-toxic preservative, and bought sheds will usually have been treated prior to sale. Depending on the size of building, the roof will shed considerable amounts of rainwater. A water butt to collect this water is always a good idea.

Contrasting & associating materials: Sheds should be simply sited and suitably screened with trellis, hedging, fencing, walling, or a combination of any of these. Close to a house, a shed and utility area could be designed to form an extension of the architecture. Next to a path, a shed can play host to overhead beams, covered with climbers, that will both soften its outline and blend it into the wider garden.

GREENHOUSES

Characteristics: Glass-sided and glass-roofed buildings providing a warm environment, protection for tender plants in winter, and suitable conditions for propagation, growing on, and a multitude of other horticultural activities. Traditionally set in the vegetable garden, many greenhouses are attractive enough to become focal points in their own right, and merit a more prominent position in the composition. Careful siting is crucial – as with any small building, there is a tendency to plonk greenhouses down anywhere, which can spell disaster in a well-conceived design.

Greenhouses are normally rectangular, but there are other shapes and styles available; hexagonal and circular houses will create interesting design possibilities for the areas around them, and lean-to greenhouses can fit neatly against a wall. Like sheds, greenhouses need good paths for access, and ample hardstanding around them. For a heated greenhouse, electric power lines from the nearest source will need to be buried safely in a conduit. Paraffin heaters provide a cheaper form of heating, but they require regular maintenance and can be hazardous if knocked over.

Uses: All the above, but also for growing specialist plants such as cacti, alpines, vines, orchids, as well as tomatoes, herbs in winter, pot flowers for the house, and tender or unusual species.

Construction: Greenhouses are usually constructed from either timber or metal alloy. While the first often look better and more substantial, owing to the thicker sizing of the framework, the latter usually last a good deal longer. Timber houses can be built from either hardwood or softwood (cedar is popular), but all will need regular treatment with non-toxic preservative. Both types of house must be positioned on an absolutely horizontal base, to prevent the frame from twisting, which would lead to difficulties fitting the glass subsequently. This base usually consists of a number of courses of brickwork, on to which the frame is bolted.

Contrasting & associating materials: Gravel can form an excellent surround, as can brushed aggregate concrete. Greenhouses can be planned as focal points in either the vegetable garden or the decorative garden, with the composition radiating from them.

The greenhouse is almost incidental in this profusion of planting. This makes sense as metal greenhouses can look rather austere in many settings, requiring the softening influence either of plants or of some kind of screening.

Using a greenhouse to grow plants that would not survive in the open garden can be enormously satisfying. The chance to build up a collection of well-ordered pots and containers only adds to the pleasure.

TREEHOUSES

There is a justifiable element of trickery here as both the treehouse and the enormous supporting branches of the tree below it are held up with substantial metal poles set in concrete. The overall result is superb.

Characteristics: The best treehouses are for grown-ups – I once had dinner in a fully blown dining-room 12m (40ft) up in the branches of a huge chestnut tree. Built by a professional carpenter, it was large enough to hold a dozen people and had a built-in sink, dishwasher and fridge. It was interesting to be up there in a high wind! The steps up to it were terrifying; the way down less so, particularly after a good meal and a few glasses of claret.

More typical, less sophisticated affairs are ideal for kids. These should always be sturdily built, with safety in mind, in a large tree that is absolutely sound. The most basic treehouse is simply a stout platform, reached either by climbing the tree itself, or via a rope ladder. A more elaborate one may have walls and a roof, with an adjoining staircase.

Uses: For all kinds of play activities; for children and grown-ups alike.

Construction: Invariably of timber, treehouses should be adequately sized and securely fixed. There is always an element of risk in such a situation, so the sounder the construction and the safer the access, the better it will be for everyone. Do not build a treehouse unless you have a substantial tree – there will inevitably be some damage, with a few boughs cut back and nails driven in. Most people will be able to tackle such a project, and it can be ideal for kids, with the correct supervision.

Contrasting & associating materials: The most spectacular treehouses can become focal points; more often, they will blend comfortably into an orchard or spinney.

PLAYHOUSES

The local gang hanging out at their favourite joint, and enjoying it too! Solid logs make an excellent material for building playhouses and, if they are well constructed, such buildings should last a lifetime.

Characteristics: At their best, these are magical places, often made by children themselves or an enlightened grown-up. While safety must always be a consideration, the best playhouses are often ramshackle affairs, built from materials to hand, and readily demolished on a whim or in a high wind. Children naturally like to hide away, and the fact that the playhouses are usually hidden from view is probably just as well, for they are no architectural masterpieces. The argument that such structures should be in full view of the kitchen window is nonsense, certainly as far as the children are concerned.

At their worst, playhouses come in the form of horrible plastic Wendy houses, and are filled with ready-made toys that leave not an ounce of imagination to the child. The simplest approach, which can be the best, is just to cast a sheet over a clothes-line, climbing frame or other piece of play equipment. Such tents can be quickly modified, and are retrievable in case of rain.

Uses: Imaginative play.

Construction: Timber is the favourite material, with the addition of anything else that comes readily to hand. Ideally, playhouses should be sound, but with the potential for expansion. Purpose-built houses, like purpose-built gardens, tend to appeal less to the child; they are less flexible, last indefinitely, and end up as follies in later life.

Contrasting & associating materials: The best playhouses are hidden away, and so do not associate with anything much. Probably this is the best way.

PLAY EQUIPMENT

Characteristics: Although you can move some of the lighter play equipment around, major elements will, to all intents and purposes, be fixed in one position for a considerable length of time.

The choice is wide: swings, slides, climbing frames, see-saws, sandpits or sandboxes, and so on. Many of these can be bought ready-made, but prices and sturdiness will vary enormously, and as a general rule, you get what you pay for. Bent metal equipment, although relatively cheap, is neither attractive nor particularly long-lasting, especially if there are several boisterous children using it. There is, on the other hand, an increasing amount of really excellent timber equipment coming on to the market, including wonderful forts and other buildings. These look handsome and really do stand up to an enormous amount of wear, and some have slides and climbing frames built into them. Most of these units are modular, so you can extend the play area over a period of time.

As a general rule, try to group equipment in one area. This will contain the inevitably busy outline of the pieces and allow a watchful eye to be concentrated in one place.

Do not forget the obvious potential of features you already have in the garden. A strong branch is an obvious candidate for a swing, while stout lengths of logs can be arranged and fixed in various patterns to create fascinating climbing structures; large-diameter logs can be set upright in the ground to form aerial stepping stones; ropes slung from tree to tree can be great for climbing across or used for swinging across a stream;

sand play areas of all shapes and sizes can be easily introduced. In other words, always bear safety in mind but use your imagination; the results will be great fun for all concerned.

Uses: Play!

Construction: It is particularly important to fix bought equipment firmly, as it is often light and tips over easily. Always follow the manufacturer's instructions, and if necessary err on the side of caution, where jobs like setting legs in concrete are concerned. Timber equipment should also be firmly fixed, usually in concrete foundations. Remember, the more comprehensive the equipment, the more children will come and play on it, and the more safety-conscious you need to be.

Much of the equipment can, however, be made at home, and timber again will be the obvious choice. Hardwoods are usually more durable than soft, and generously sized, sturdy timbers are essential. Beware splinters on any wood, particularly on rougher surfaces such as railway sleepers. Always finish things off as smoothly as possible with sandpaper. Non-toxic preservative should be applied to all wooden equipment at regular intervals. Straightforward carpentry skills are all that is required, and these are projects in which the kids will be delighted to become involved!

You need also to think about the ground underneath the play equipment. Grass is soft but wears out quickly; perhaps the best surface is a thick layer of chipped bark

I wish I had been able to enjoy such a cleverly constructed play area when I was a child! This is an excellent example of a well-thought-out, well-integrated and sturdy design that not only looks good, but also works well and is bound to get plenty of use.

contained within a framework of boards. This is both easy on the knees and looks unobtrusive.

Contrasting & associating materials: Play areas tend to look best in the more informal parts of the garden,

where there is more likely to be ample room to run around and generally make chaos. A background of planting and a surround of lawn is all that is needed. A shed or somewhere else to store toys, bikes and all the rest, is invaluable.

RAISED BEDS

The curve of this raised bed is echoed by the circular paving pattern of granite setts that adjoins it. The bed is constructed from stout logs set into the ground at slightly varying heights, with planting encouraged to grow over the edge to soften the line. Similar logs, specifically for this purpose and pre-treated against rot, are widely available.

Characteristics: Raised beds can be both practical and attractive in virtually any garden. They bring planting up to an easy working height, which can be particularly useful for people who are handicapped. Raising plants closer to eye level makes them look more mature and means that small species such as alpines can also be enjoyed more easily. Most beds will be rectangular in outline, blending naturally with terraced and architectural areas close to the house, as well as with steps and changes in level.

Materials will include most of those used for boundaries, and will take their cue from the surrounding garden and locality. Timber can also be used on its own, in the form of heavy baulks such as railway sleepers, or, where load-bearing is a consideration (as on a roof garden), by using boards for the sides of beds. Sleepers are particularly useful and, because of their weight, they can be bedded on a foundation of well-compacted soil, making sure they are absolutely level. They are best laid horizontally in courses, or cut down to about half their length and set vertically close together in the ground. This vertical treatment is highly suitable for logs, and paving slabs, too, can be set upright and bedded securely in concrete. However, they tend to look very hard, and need plenty of softening with prostrate plants to flop down over the edges.

Uses: Raised beds provide a useful growing space for a wide range of plants, including shrubs, herbaceous perennials, alpines, annuals, bulbs and, not least, vegetables and herbs. They are ideal for places where it is impossible to plant directly into the ground, such as a completely paved courtyard, balcony, or roof garden. An added advantage is that it becomes possible to introduce a specific soil type that might not be present in the wider garden, allowing you to grow ericaceous or other specialist plants.

Construction: Walling materials, such as brick or stone, will need foundations that are twice the width of the walls. Good drainage is essential if the bed is not to become waterlogged, and as the walls are built, pipes should be inserted just above the surrounding ground level, spaced 900mm (3ft) apart, to drain away excess water. If the bed sits on earth, the ground should first be forked over, and a 150mm (6in) layer of hardcore or broken stone laid on top. A layer of turf should then be placed upside down over the hardcore, and at least 450mm (18in) of clean topsoil for the planting. This may need topping up after six months or so, to compensate for settling. If the bed is built on a hard surface, a 150mm (6in) layer of hardcore or crushed stone should be placed on the bottom and the soil built up as above.

Railway sleepers can be laid in a staggered bond like bricks, and, for additional stability, should be drilled to accept steel reinforcing rods which can be driven well into the ground. Raised beds constructed with board sides will need a protective lining of some kind. At its simplest, this will be black plastic sheeting stapled to the inside, but for a longer life, fibreglass boxes, with drainage holes in the bottom, can be made up to fit individual beds.

Raised beds make a useful feature on a roof garden. These should be filled with a lightweight soil mix placed over a sheet of geo-textile and a drainage layer of clay granules.

Contrasting & associating materials: This will once again depend on the immediate garden surroundings. Brick or stone beds may echo similar materials elsewhere, while the darker colour of railway sleepers will set up a dramatic contrast with pale gravels and pale pre-cast concrete slabs. Boards can be painted or stained to pick up a surrounding colour scheme, and will link naturally with timber decking.

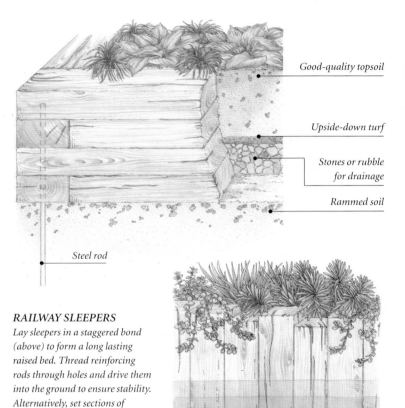

Good-quality topsoil

Upside-down turf

Stones or rubble
for drainage

Rammed soil

Steel rod

In this strongly linear pattern, the raised beds and paving naturally lead the eye down to the informal seating area beneath the tree at the far end. Both pergola and planting are superbly generous, forming a magical tunnel.

RAILWAY SLEEPERS

Lay sleepers in a staggered bond (above) to form a long lasting raised bed. Thread reinforcing rods through holes and drive them into the ground to ensure stability. Alternatively, set sections of sleepers vertically at different heights (right) to form a rhythmical design.

Sleepers haunched in
concrete or rammed soil

SLAB PLANTER

Use paving slabs positioned side by side and firmly set in concrete for a low-cost planter.

Bull-nosed brick

BRICK PLANTER

Build a brick raised bed to echo brickwork used in the house or elsewhere in the garden. A bull-nosed coping looks attractive and is comfortable to sit on. Weep pipes prevent the soil from becoming waterlogged.

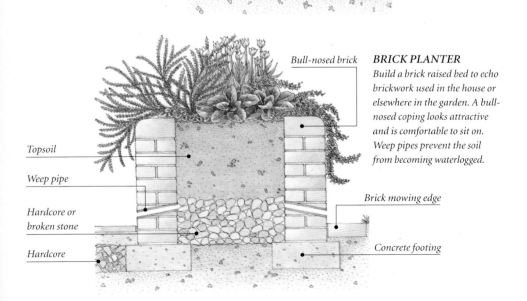

Topsoil

Weep pipe

Hardcore or
broken stone

Hardcore

Brick mowing edge

Concrete footing

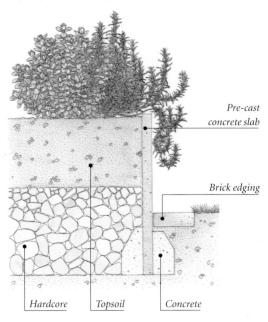

Pre-cast
concrete slab

Brick edging

Hardcore   Topsoil   Concrete

BUILT-IN SEATING

This is an excellent example of a dual-purpose feature in which the seat doubles up as a retaining wall holding back the higher ground to the left. Such a feature provides a powerful design element, the curve of the seat subtly leading the eye towards the grass path and the area beyond, with a further echo in the adjoining paving.

Characteristics: Built-in seating can be used in many situations, as a space-saving feature that can be incorporated into a totally designed outside living environment. Seats can be built into the right angle formed by two walls or raised beds, constructed as an extension to a barbecue or water feature, or designed as an integral part of a flight of steps.

Timber is often used for construction, and this is easily worked to virtually any pattern or shape, and can even be designed with a hinged top to provide storage space within. Materials are often combined: a brick or stone base, for example, can be run out from an adjoining feature or wall of the same material, and given a timber top. It could also be topped with pre-cast concrete slabs or other type of paving.

In the wider garden, seats built around trees can be used to provide good focal points. Many ready-made designs are unnecessarily fussy, with multi-faceted sides; it is perfectly possible to build seats to your own design in simple square or rectangular shapes, making them big enough to double up as seat, table, lounger and play surface. You will occasionally see delightful metal seats, made from shaped steel or iron similar to that used in park fences; these are still available but expensive. If you inherit one, it will be well worth repairing.

Uses: As seats, obviously, but also as focal points, loungers, and play surfaces.

Construction: There is a wide choice of suitable materials, with timber being the most commonly used. A brick or stone base must be built off suitable foundations. Where a seat is worked into a flight of steps, it can be incorporated to one side, to run into surrounding planting, or the edge of a lawn, pool or other feature. The seat will be an extension of a tread, 30–45cm (12–18in) high, and could be fronted with paving of some kind to echo that used close by. A seat round a tree should be generous in its proportions, perhaps 2.5m (8ft) or even 3m (10ft) square. All timber seating can be constructed using straightforward carpentry skills, whereas metal seats will need to be made by a craftsman blacksmith.

Contrasting & associating materials: Seats are usually built as an extension of the features that they adjoin, being built from the same materials. This should provide a natural harmony in either a traditional or a more contemporary situation.

WOODEN SEATING AROUND A TREE

A large seat will allow for a range of activities, but keep the basic framework in proportion to the tree it surrounds.

Nail or screw slats on top of the framework, being careful to leave adequate growing space around the tree trunk.

BARBECUES

What charisma! Here is the ultimate example of one-upmanship in barbecuing. The barbecue itself appears to have been constructed in a thoroughly practical way from part of an old chimney.

Characteristics: You either are, or are not a barbecue fanatic, but should you be one of those who cannot resist the attraction of alfresco eating, then a built-in barbecue may be just the thing for you. The advantage over a portable model is sheer size; you can build something to feed half the neighbourhood, if necessary, instead of cooking in endless rotation and never getting a meal yourself! It also allows you to design the barbecue either as an island feature, allowing circulation around it, or against a wall or other feature; and to provide for ample worktops and storage space, along with integrated seating.

A barbecue can provide a focus for an outside living and entertaining area, becoming part of a carefully considered composition of built-in seating, raised beds, overhead beams and planting, the latter including herbs to flavour the cooking.

The siting of a barbecue needs to be thought about carefully, in relation to prevailing winds, afternoon and evening sun, and the proximity to your kitchen. Do not forget your neighbours either; there is nothing more annoying than smoke pouring over the fence into your garden.

Uses: In summer, barbecues are purely for cooking, although built-in storage can be useful for all kinds of things! In winter, the cooking grids can be removed and the various split level areas will make excellent platforms for pots, which will always brighten a hard-landscaped area.

Construction: Materials for construction need to be durable, so brick and stone are both common and practical choices, while reconstituted stone, rendered and *in situ* concrete can also be used. Grids for cooking, and charcoal trays, can either be bought in kit form, or fabricated by a blacksmith or welder. Stainless steel is more expensive than other materials, but it is also the most durable and the easiest to keep clean.

Foundations for walls need to be soundly constructed, while timberwork for store doors or adjoining seats will require basic carpentry skills. Charcoal is the most commonly used fuel, but you can build space for bottled or natural gas, or electric units, into a purpose-designed housing. For the last two, this will also mean laying feeder pipes or cables (to a suitable safety standard), usually below surrounding paving. Advanced barbecues, for serious chefs, may also have chimneys, incorporating dampers and various other devices for controlling the draught.

Contrasting & associating materials: The design of the barbecue, as well as the materials used for its construction, should be consistent with those found in the surrounding garden.

CONSTRUCTING A BUILT-IN BARBECUE
Brick is by far the most adaptable and practical material for building a barbecue and this design incorporates both storage and an adjoining seat.

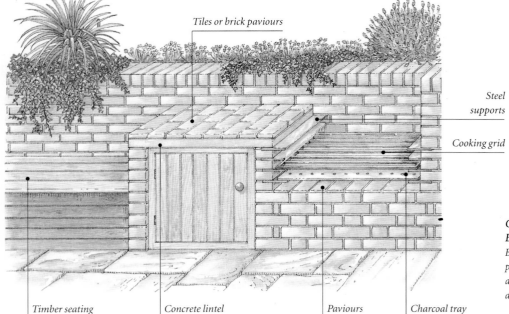

Tiles or brick paviours

Steel supports

Cooking grid

Timber seating

Concrete lintel

Paviours

Charcoal tray

The furnishing of a garden brings life and personality to the space. Choosing ornaments is highly personal but it is precisely this expression of individuality that sets one garden apart from another.

Cost is, of course, an important factor, and just as with your furniture inside the home, this can vary enormously. As with most things, you get what you pay for. Keep things simple and do not get carried away by the latest craze in an up-market store – you can probably buy the same thing, or something better, at half the price elsewhere. Also, bear in mind that not everything needs to be shop-bought. Many of the best features or ornaments can simply be 'found objects'. An old and twisted sun-bleached log can be smothered with a clematis, and set as a focal point at the turn of a path, or act as an occasional seat within the paving of a terrace.

Some homes and gardens are full of every conceivable ornament; some are sparse but stunningly elegant – most fall between the two extremes. As with the majority of design matters, it is best to be understated and to resist the urge to buy on impulse, unless you find something that is just right for a certain situation.

Your choice of ornament and furniture plays a key role in reinforcing the style of your garden. For example, a contemporary garden will readily accept clean, modern pieces, whether these be pots, urns, furniture or anything else. A classical garden suggests a more traditional approach. Added to this is a sensitive use of materials. Stone may look good with terracotta or a traditional lead sink, but would sit uncomfortably with hi-tech plastic or fibreglass. In other words, it is important to think about both the relationship of materials and that between shapes and spaces.

Like plants, pots look better in odd-numbered than in even groupings: three, five, seven and nine look better than two, four, six and eight. Remember also that your garden is constantly evolving, and that ornament and furniture can be readily moved, which allows the garden to take on an entirely new persona.

Garden furniture, unfortunately, is frequently designed to look good rather than be comfortable, so try before you buy! Comfort should, I believe, come first, followed closely by a style that fits with the rest of the garden. The principles of choosing furniture are the same as for ornament – there is a clear difference between a deck chair or bean bag and the formality of a stone seat or classic timber bench. Each of these categories will sit comfortably within gardens that reflect these styles.

Overall, your choice of ornament and furnishing is a matter of personal taste. As with other areas of garden design, simplicity combined with a sensitive consideration of environment is a reliable recipe for success.

Above: *Seats and furniture will bring personal taste and character to an outdoor room, so choose them carefully. This curved seat could reflect the underlying floorplan or the shape of adjacent planted areas.*

Left: *This eclectic mix of materials creates real individuality, along with dazzling colour that really brings this dull wall alive. Imagination is the key to successful design.*

Opposite: *Ornament does not have to be expensive or sophisticated to be effective. Here, two tall, simple wooden structures possess as much presence as highly crafted sculptures, and fit more naturally with the rural setting.*

STATUARY

Good statuary, as with much hard landscaping, can often be enhanced by a frame or the softening influence of planting. While there is humour here, there is also a fair degree of manipulation, or perhaps good luck! Regular pruning, or slight adjustments to the position of the statue, will be required to keep this composition under control.

While this could be used as a topiary frame, it is also valid when used as a statue in its own right. The best setting for such a piece will almost certainly be an informal one, *to mimic the natural habitat of the animal, and while the immediate surroundings are of prime importance, lighting could also be used to dramatic effect.*

Standing stones possess enormous power and drama. Their individual nature means that some will look perfect in a natural setting, while others can suit hi-tech surroundings.

Characteristics: Statues have been with us for a very long time, and were just as much at home in classic Roman outdoor rooms as they are in a contemporary garden. But beauty is in the eye of the beholder, and while the most perfectly modelled bust will appeal to some, an anguished arrangement of sculpted steel may turn on others. Of course the style and situation of the garden should influence the choice, but remember that a formal layout can be traditional or modern, and will ask for statues that are chosen accordingly.

Although figures are a common choice, statues can mimic virtually anything: animals, fish, birds and even garden gnomes, so popular in England. The last should not be written off, however much they are condemned by horticultural snobs; a sense of humour is one of the most important elements in any garden, so to hell with what the establishment says!

Uses: Statues can be used as greater or lesser focal points, drawing the eye to a particular point in the garden. Their placing will therefore need careful thought, and this will often have been worked out on the drawing-board at the design stage. Statues demand attention in their own right but can also be used to give emphasis to another feature: surrounding or providing the central feature of a pool; standing in niches along the face of a wall or hedge; or flanking a doorway.

Construction: Most sculpture will be carved or cast by specialists (though this is an area where even children can create an object of worth), and materials can include natural or reconstituted stone, concrete, timber, metal and synthetics, such as plastic or fibreglass, or even osier. Most will be static, but some will be plumbed for water spouts, or powered as moving features.

Contrasting & associating materials: This will be entirely dependent on the setting, though a fabulous bronze or subtle wood carving may look equally at home with both natural and man-made surfaces. Perhaps more than with anything else in the garden, this is a question of what looks and feels right. In short, it will test your eye as a creative and sensitive person.

WALL PLAQUES

The choice of any kind of ornament is a highly individual matter, and objects often carry with them a whole collection of personal associations or even religious overtones. Great care and attention should always be taken when siting an ornamental feature; this marble plaque stands out in sharp contrast to the brick wall around it.

Characteristics: These appear in an enormous range of styles, patterns, sizes and shapes, from huge carvings in relief, set into the walls of an historic garden, to a child's school project that will give no less pleasure to the viewer. They are found all over the world, and often have a strong ethnic character. Although wall plaques tend to be popular subjects for bringing back home from holiday, it is worth remembering that what looks spectacular in one situation may look uncomfortable in another.

Uses: Like statues, plaques provide a focal point, but usually at a higher level. Being mounted on the face of a wall they naturally bring interest to the vertical plane, and can be used either singly or as a group to set up a particular pattern. They can also be fitted with a spout, allowing water to fall into a pool or bowl below.

Construction: Plaques can be made from a wide range of materials that include stone, reconstituted stone, wood, synthetics, ceramics, metal and glass. The most complicated are craftsman-made, but simpler ceramics or carvings can be more easily constructed. Where water is used, they can be plumbed to a submersible pump in the pool or bowl below.

Contrasting & associating materials: There is a suitable plaque for every conceivable situation and associating material, so choose carefully.

OBELISKS

Characteristics: One of the most dramatic focal points of all, shaped like an upside-down exclamation mark and designed to draw the eye. The classic obelisk usually takes the form of a tapered stone needle, standing on top of four balls, which are in turn positioned on a rectangular stone base. The largest are built as monuments, and are only successful in parkland, but there are many different variations in size and form, and you should be able to find an obelisk that will suit even the smallest garden.

Uses: Positioned singly as a focal point at the end of a vista, walk or pergola. Pairs can be set to flank gates or doorways, or a number can be positioned on either side of a pathway in much the same way as topiary shapes, when they will have the effect of accelerating the view towards its end.

Construction: Obelisks are usually constructed from natural or reconstituted stone, but the shape can be elegantly created using virtually any hard material as well as by clipped and trained hedging plants such as yews. Obelisks can also be constructed from specially designed trellis structures, the base taking the form of a square tub into which climbers can be planted.

Contrasting & associating materials: Obelisks are adaptable features, and while they will fit naturally into a traditional or formal garden, the larger examples can also look at home in the most informal parkland setting. Because of their simple geometry, they can also be highly effective in a contemporary design, especially where they are associated with traditional materials such as natural stone, brick and gravel, although they will also look good positioned next to high-quality pre-cast concrete paving.

Although obelisks are often used singly, this little tribe is rather fun and highly individualistic. With any kind of ornamentation, positioning is all important, and these look just right nestling into the edge of the informal planting. The construction used here is unusual, and was almost certainly carried out using materials to hand.

URNS

The beauty of a well-chosen and carefully positioned urn is that it will look good throughout the year, even in the depths of winter. This stone urn has been set alongside a whole family of compatible features, including a clipped box, ivy-clad columns and trompe l'œil trellis.

Is this contemporary urn broken or not? Either way it provides an attractive focal point and is undoubtedly a highly personal, possibly home-made, piece. Such ornaments are full of a character and charm that is unique to their owners.

Characteristics: Most urns are classical in design, and are available in a vast range of patterns and sizes. Depending on size, they are more or less suitable for planting, but often look their best when left empty. They usually stand on a base or pedestal.

Uses: Urns are often used as focal points in a formal setting, and can be positioned singly, in pairs, or groups, or flanking a door, arch, path or pergola. If they are to be planted, the larger the bowl the better, to allow for adequate root development and needing less frequent watering.

Construction: Lead was traditional, albeit expensive, and is still used today, but usually now of stone or reconstituted stone. Cast iron was formerly a popular material.

Fibreglass and plastic have their uses, but are simply degrading when they are used to imitate another material. Concrete urns usually look cheap, although recently there have been a number of new processes that produce a more realistic surface texture that is far more acceptable.

Contrasting & associating materials: Generally speaking, classical urns sit comfortably with most other traditional materials such as natural paving, brick, gravel, and good-quality pre-cast concrete slabs. Soft landscaping, in the form of planting, lawns and background hedges, will also create a worthwhile setting.

FOUND OBJECTS

This collection of collected objects is enormous fun, and will certainly be unique. You should always endeavour to create a garden that reflects your own personal taste, rather than slavishly following the dictates of horticultural snobs.

Characteristics: These can be fun and inexpensive, and are things that will reflect your personality and sense of humour. They will also, in all probability, be unique. The term covers a miscellaneous range of items, from a gnarled old log, a coal scuttle, or rugged boulder, to a set of beautifully reflective glass balls that were originally used as floats for commercial fishing nets. In short, they will be anything that catches your eye and can be used as a point of interest, somewhere in the garden.

Uses: As a major or incidental focal point, which must always be positioned with care, even if appearing not to be. Depending on the object, use might be decorative, or more practical: a log or boulder doubling as a seat, a hollowed out stone as a birdbath, a coal scuttle as a planter or a bathtub as a herb garden.

Construction: The real point is that these objects are found and subsequently used without any interference by you.

Contrasting & associating materials: Depending on the feature, the choices are legion. An old log can sit as comfortably in woodland as on a crisp concrete terrace. Use your imagination and sensitivity.

The power and movement in this superbly gnarled old log is supreme and introduces a completely different theme to the well-planted terrace. It serves several purposes, as a seat, a children's climbing frame, and ultimately as a fine piece of sculpture. The only problem here will have been the difficulty of lifting it into position.

STONE

While stone baskets of fruit are commonplace, baskets of flints are rather more unusual, but certainly no less attractive. Impressive containers can be filled with almost anything that appeals, so use your imagination and look beyond standard ideas.

Characteristics: Stone and reconstituted stone containers can be found in a wide range of designs, usually traditional, but sometimes modern. They will range from heavily carved or modelled troughs and containers with a classical feel, to the utter simplicity of old stone sinks that were used for domestic purposes and for farm animals. While the first tend to look best in formal settings, the second will fit comfortably into less structured designs.

Slate water tanks were often used to collect rainwater, and if repaired make deep and wonderful containers, while some of the largest stone troughs, which were used for crushing cider apples, are large enough to contain a substantial collection of plants.

Uses: Classical patterns are always at home in formal gardens, flanking entrances, acting as focal points, or helping to provide a balance for a regular pattern of beds and borders. Any container is useful where there is no available open ground for planting, but should be as deep and generous as possible. Sinks and agricultural stone containers often provide a cool growing area for specialist collections of small plants, such as alpines. Sinks can also become attractive small pools or water features, and some, originally used for juice extraction, have lips that will allow water to fall into another container below.

Construction: Reconstituted stone containers are cast from moulds, while natural stone is crafted by hand. Both require skilled labour.

Contrasting & associating materials: Both formal pieces and less formal sinks will relate well to natural stone or good-quality pre-cast concrete slabs, gravel and brick, along with grass and other soft landscaping.

Slate is a beautiful material that can be crafted into a vast range of different containers and patterns. Here the odd crack simply adds to the character of the piece, while the colour of the planting provides the perfect foil both to the slate and the white window and walls behind.

CERAMIC

These pots, with their distinctly Mediterranean influence, bring a splash of colour and a strong sense of movement to this setting and the bright planting has been chosen to suit their vibrant patterns. The containers have been raised from the ground to aid drainage.

Characteristics: Ceramic containers are becoming increasingly available, mostly from overseas, though there are several excellent English designers producing beautiful items. Chinese bowls are popular, as are those from the Mediterranean, but not all will be frost-proof. The beauty of ceramics lies in their surface patterning and colour, which can be dramatic or subtle. The larger containers will be free-standing, but smaller pieces are often designed to be hung on a wall. All pots must have a drainage hole, and it is a good idea to assist drainage on a paved area by standing them on specially moulded feet.

Uses: As their resistance to frost may be uncertain, it may be sensible to move these containers inside the house or conservatory during the winter. This being so, you could plant them with non-hardy species that will flourish outside in summer. As with any container, the larger the better, and a lightweight soil mix will make moving them easier.

Construction: This is a craftsman potter's job, and the higher the firing temperature the more durable the pot will be.

Contrasting & associating materials: Brightly coloured ceramics are vibrant and often look at their best in a contemporary design where other colours and different materials are freely used. If containers are hung on an outside wall, the wall (as well as any continuous inside walls) could be painted to pick up on the colour range of the containers.

Considerable thought has gone into co-ordinating this composition, and each element has been positioned with care and sensitivity. The deep blue glaze of the pots harmonizes perfectly with the ceramic tiles of the swimming pool.

TERRACOTTA

These wonderful organic shapes are placed over rhubarb to force the early stems into growth. They are almost too handsome to be hidden away in the vegetable patch and there is no reason why they could not be used to force rhubarb in more ornamental parts of the garden.

Characteristics: Terracotta has a long pedigree, and comes originally from the Mediterranean areas. One of the best-known and most popular materials for pots and containers, its clay base allows it to be moulded to virtually any pattern. Pots, troughs, window boxes and urns can all be found, with some urns commanding high prices at auction. With age, terracotta acquires a distinct patina that adds to its charm. I have pots of this kind that have been in use for over twenty years, the odd chip simply adding to their character.

Some of the finest containers come from Crete. These *pithoi* were originally storage jars, but are now increasingly made for export.

Uses: The natural colours of the clay make terracotta an ideal foil for planting, and as a rule, the larger the pot the happier the plants will be. They will have a cool root-run and the soil will dry out less quickly. Beware of plastic imitations that,

apart from being aesthetically dishonest, do not have the same cooling influence. The largest pots or urns can look effective if they are left unplanted and used as a focal point at the end of a vista or path. Smaller pots, of the same or varying size, look delightful set in groups on a paved area or flight of steps.

Construction: If you are a potter, you can throw your own. There are marvellous garden pots being made, most of which are manufactured in Mediterranean countries. Always check with suppliers that they are frost-proof. If they are not, they will crack and flake away in cold, damp winters. If in doubt, bring them indoors or swathe them in straw or bubble plastic during the winter.

Contrasting & associating materials: Terracotta is an extremely adaptable material, and will look equally at home in a mellow courtyard, formal garden or contemporary setting.

Terracotta becomes more and more beautiful with age. This superb urn was once painted, and the peeling surface now only adds to its character. Raising an ornament to eye level often has the effect of throwing it into sharper relief, thus increasing its impact.

PRE-CAST CONCRETE

Concrete can be cast and finished in an extraordinarily varied range of finishes. This large pot has been cast in situ straight on to a base of stone, which it closely resembles.

Such a deep pot will provide ample room for a plant to spread its roots, and if it is sited in a lightly shaded place, should not require very frequent watering.

Shallow containers make the perfect choice for a selection of alpine plants, as many species appreciate the dry conditions that are usually created as a result of this type

of design. In this example, the pale colour of the concrete provides a pleasing contrast to the darker grey of the railway sleepers on which the container is standing.

Characteristics: Concrete is one of the most versatile materials in the garden, and as it can be cast into virtually any shape or pattern, it can also be used for pots and containers. These may be huge, such as sections of large-diameter drainpipe, which can be used as raised beds, right down to small bowls of the simplest design. Excellent examples of containers cast *in situ* can be found on the European continent and on the west coast of the United States, where they are often used to extend the hard landscape.

Surface textures can vary, according to the type of aggregate selected, from a smooth, virtually polished finish, to one in which the aggregate in the mix is exposed to provide a rough and marbled finish. Ribbed and moulded patterns are also possible. As with anything to do with design, the character of the material should be respected; there is little point in using concrete to ape another material, though concrete quickly weathers down to resemble natural stone.

Uses: For plants, water, or as focal points. Containers cast *in situ* can be used as extensions to a terrace, to flank the edge of a hard landscape area, or to extend the line of a well-detailed flight of concrete steps in a contemporary setting. They would also be a logical choice to extend the line of a house built from concrete out into the surrounding landscape.

Construction: In situ containers will require wooden or ply shuttering, and skilled help. Most moveable containers will be bought from manufacturers or garden centres. The deeper and wider the pot, the better for planting.

Contrasting & associating materials: Although concrete is a contemporary material, it will blend into a wide range of settings depending on the style of design. As a general rule, concrete pots will look most comfortable within a crisp contemporary setting alongside pre-cast concrete paving, railway sleepers and gravel.

METAL

Plain metal buckets make terrific containers and have an unfussy, clean appearance that will not detract from your chosen planting. Drill a few holes in the base of new buckets for drainage – older buckets may already have rusted through.

Lead is a particularly beautiful material, which looks better and better as it weathers, and this fine old lead sink bears a date and the initials of the original owner. As the container is so large, the planting should not require constant watering.

Characteristics: Metal is a versatile material and has considerable potential for containers in the garden. Historical pieces were often made from beautifully crafted lead, rich with patterning, and often bearing the coat-of-arms of the garden owners, together with the date. But there are some stunning contemporary designs being produced in all kinds of different metals and finishes.

Many metal containers will have started life as something else: copper or cast-iron washing boilers are large and practical, simply needing holes drilled in the bottom for drainage, while coal scuttles, iron or copper, make smaller but useful pots. Old bathtubs, galvanized buckets (which are sometimes painted to imitate those used on barges), milk churns, old cattle or horse mangers, and bowls of various kinds, will all be suitable. Remember that the pot quite often becomes incidental to the plant or plants in them, and it will be the plants that are the real stars.

Uses: For plants, or sometimes used empty as a dramatic focal point. A large, sound container can be used for a water feature.

Construction: Invariably a skilled metal-working job. Repairs will need to be carried out by an experienced blacksmith or welder.

Contrasting & associating materials: Fine old lead cisterns will be perfectly at home in a formal garden with traditional materials, while contemporary designs will look fine in a far more hi-tech situation, possibly combined with plastics, fibreglass and other crisp, visually clean surfaces such as railway sleepers or decking. As usual, match the container to the situation.

TIMBER

PLASTIC & FIBREGLASS

Large timber boxes of this kind can be bought in pieces and then assembled and positioned in the garden. Once filled with soil, such containers will be difficult to move, but their ample proportions can accommodate even rampant climbers.

This arresting fibreglass pot makes a terrific statement, and proves that when treated in an innovative way, even the most mundane subject can become a major focal point. Choosing planting for such a pot might present quite a challenge.

Characteristics: Timber is one of the most easily worked materials, and so the range of containers is almost limitless. Classical patterns, such as Versailles tubs, have a long history, and are perfect for a formal garden, while an old half-barrel, painted black and white, is ideal by the front door of a cottage. Colour, as well as protecting the surface can be used to link with an overall theme, or with overhead beams or decking. Window boxes bring plants into the vertical plane, and their use is often the only gardening option open to flat or apartment dwellers. As timber is relatively light, when filled with an equally lightweight soil mix, it makes an excellent choice of container for a balcony or roof garden. Timber swells when wet, sealing construction joints, so containers can be used to form miniature water gardens.

Uses: As plant containers, herb and water gardens of variable size.

Construction: Timber is easily worked and can be tailored to fit awkward situations, such as window openings or alcoves. Hardwoods are more durable than softwoods, but the latter can be pressure-treated prior to purchase, or regularly treated with a non-toxic preservative.

Contrasting & associating materials: Timber obviously has an affinity with other woodwork , whether this be decking, overheads, or raised beds built from railway sleepers. The potential of paint colour opens up possibilities for both harmony and sharp contrast with a surrounding scheme. As a rule, timber is a forgiving material, blending easily into a wide range of situations.

Characteristics: Plastic and fibreglass are among the most misused and abused materials of the twentieth century. They have enormous potential for creating fresh organic shapes in wonderful colours, but that very versatility is so often used only to imitate other surfaces.

Any material should be used honestly and with integrity; to create a fibreglass pastiche of an old lead cistern, or a fine classical stone urn in plastic, is visually outrageous and aesthetic sacrilege. Synthetics are strong, rot-proof and virtually indestructible. Used properly, they can be an asset; used improperly, they are merely an environmental problem. The real strength of these materials is that they can be moulded in the widest range of shapes, particularly fluid and free-form patterns. Colour is no problem, from subtle pastels to vibrant primaries. Pots can be made in virtually any size, often designed to stack or interlock together. They can be used either at ground level, as window boxes or hanging containers, as well as for planting or for water, for which, being rot-proof, they are ideal.

Uses: For the widest range of pots and containers in contemporary designs. Naturally forming focal points, they are suitable either for plants or water. The material is light so is useful where load-bearing is a problem, particularly on roof gardens.

Construction: Moulded by specialist manufacturers. Unless you are an expert in the manufacture of fibreglass, these are items you will purchase.

Contrasting & associating materials: Almost exclusively alongside crisp, modern materials in a contemporary setting.

CAST & WROUGHT IRON

This highly detailed, matching set of garden furniture has a wonderfully regal air about it. Metal can be a cold material to sit on, but a few cushions will help to soften the outline in more temperate weather, perhaps co-ordinated to link with a colour scheme inside the house, as well as providing much needed comfort.

The combination of wrought iron and metal mesh in these garden rocking chairs is a fine example of traditional and contemporary techniques coming together in a way that is thoroughly practical and visually attractive. The colour blends perfectly into the garden and the seats will certainly be comfortable to sit in.

Characteristics: Cast-iron furniture was made popular by the Victorians, who produced a vast range of patterns, styles and sizes. Pieces were often made in sections and then bolted together, sometimes entirely of iron, but often with slatted timber backs and seats. Such items are heavy, which gives them visual and actual stability, but chairs can be incredibly uncomfortable and often need cushions. Today, reproduction cast-iron furniture is often made in alloy, making it lighter and less susceptible to corrosion.

Wrought iron is far more fluid in appearance, being made from strips of metal that are then joined together. Those wonderful park benches, where the ends and arms are wrought from a single spiral of material, look terrific in any garden. Designs can be infinitely varied, but try them for comfort before you buy anything. Tables often have wrought-iron bases, and timber, glass or even marble tops. It all depends on how ostentatious you want to be! Heavy-gauge bent wire is also used for items of furniture, but tends to look flimsy. Personally, I do not like it!

There are some very beautiful modern designs being created today, so keep your eyes open. The metal is usually painted, which can link with a colour scheme used elsewhere. Avoid white, which gets dirty quickly and glares in sunlight.

Uses: For tables, chairs, benches and incidental items. Benches and seats often make ideal focal points, and can be positioned accordingly.

Construction: All metalworking is a skilled job, cast items coming from a foundry, and wrought iron from a blacksmith. Blacksmiths may also carry out repairs or make items to order. Maintain metal by rubbing down and repainting.

Contrasting & associating materials: Metal furniture can be modern in design, as well as traditional, and should be chosen accordingly to blend with the overall design. Don't be seduced by fashion, or what the neighbours have, unless you really like it and it suits your garden.

This elegantly shaped and beautifully designed metal furniture sits perfectly in a contemporary roof garden to provide an excellent example of modernism at its simple best. The neat flooring, monotone planting and finely detailed screen designed to filter the force of the wind, all combine to provide a well-sheltered outdoor living space.

TIMBER

Timber is the most versatile of materials, and is relatively straightforward to work with. It can be shaped to a wide range of patterns, left plain or painted, and may either be freestanding or built directly into position. The neat and elegant design of this circular table and matching benches echo the white-painted house behind.

This stylish bench would fit comfortably into a wide range of situations, both architectural and informal, while the paint colour could be varied to suit alternative sites. The delicate and geometric design of the back slats blend particularly comfortably with the attractive tracery of branches in the background.

Simplicity is the key to the success of these benches. Black is always an excellent choice of colour as it is relatively undemonstrative and tones well with planting as well as most hard landscape materials. This type of furniture will fit into virtually any surroundings.

Characteristics: Apart from rocks, timber would have been the first material used by man for seating, and today the majority of furniture is still made from wood. The reason is simple: it is easily worked in a wide range of patterns and styles, is available in different types including hard- and softwood, and is relatively cheap. Other advantages are that it is mellow in colour and therefore does not glare in the sun, and that it ages gracefully, often with a beautiful patina.

Styles are legion, and include sets of tables and chairs, individual chairs, picnic tables with built-in seats, recliners and benches. Benches always amuse me: why do manufacturers make uncomfortably crowded three-seaters? Two-seaters are cosier, and often have a neat proportion that is not present in their larger cousins. Some designs are classic, the famous Lutyens bench being one of them. Such a seat is intended more as a focal point than a working sitting space. Humorous seats abound, with back-to-back lovers' seats and wheel-away barrow seats providing visual and practical fun.

I find much garden furniture, in whatever material, incredibly uncomfortable to sit on, so do try it out before you buy.

Uses: Often used as focal points as well as for practical purposes.

Construction: Timber is easily worked, and although you can buy sets, or single items of furniture, a competent carpenter can also make them. Both hardwood and softwood will need regular applications of preservative, or painting. You can also make basic rustic furniture out of fallen timber, although this tends to have a relatively short life and looks at its best in an informal setting. Entire tables and chairs can be cut out of single trunks with a chain saw, and these will last almost indefinitely.

Contrasting & associating materials: The enormous range of styles and colours available means that wooden furniture can be chosen to blend into virtually any situation.

STONE & RECONSTITUTED STONE

The delicacy of this flower emphasizes the rugged nature of the simple granite seat, which has been formed from three pieces of stone. The weighty slab set in front of the bench is of practical benefit, saving wear on grass or other soft surfacing.

Characteristics: Stone has long been used for outdoor furniture, either in heavily patterned classical designs, or very simply conceived with blocks for legs and slabs for tops. Shapes for seats can be curved or rectangular, while tables are also often circular. The simplest and most effective of seats can be simply made from a single smooth rock, set with care in a particular place; once in position it will be difficult to move, so it is important to get it right first time! Natural stone (which can include sandstone, slate, marble, granite and many more) is often very expensive, but infinitely variable and with superb coloration.

Reconstituted stone is popular, and far cheaper than the real thing. The best manufacturers faithfully reproduce classical designs. More imaginative contemporary pieces tend to be far less common.

Uses: Stone furniture is hard on the eye and hard to sit on, but can make a wonderful visual statement at the end of a walk, pergola or vista. Since the designs are almost always classical in inspiration, stone furniture is usually best in a formal or classical setting.

Construction: Natural stone is usually carved or shaped by craftsmen. Reconstituted stone is cast in moulds using specialist mixes, and is again usually a craft job.

Contrasting & associating materials: Classical or traditional pieces belong in similar settings, where natural stone paving, brick, gravel, grass and planting provide the ideal backdrop. Contemporary pieces, if you can find them, will associate with any of the above, but also concrete, pre-cast materials and timber, in the form of railway sleepers or decking.

PLASTIC

Well-conceived plastic-coated metal furniture can be both practical and hardwearing. These chairs have a distinctly 1950s feel about them, and certainly look as if they should be comfortable. The accompanying marble-topped table complements the seats.

Characteristics: As long as plastic furniture is designed to look like plastic, it is perfectly valid; as soon as it imitates something else, it is immediately degraded. Plastic is a naturally fluid material and is at its best when moulded into shapes that exploit this characteristic. The best-quality furniture will last for many years, and although more expensive, is usually worth the extra cost.

Advantages include lightness, durability, which allows most sets to remain outside throughout the year, and the wide range of colours in which the furniture is made. White (the most common colour) is best avoided; it not only glares in strong sun, but shows dirt easily. Most furniture of this type benefits from cushions, and these can be chosen to pick up a colourway inside the house.

Uses: Simply as furniture.

Construction: Moulded by specialist processes, plastic is sometimes also used as a protective coating to other materials such as metal, when, if carefully done, the finish can be both durable and attractive.

Contrasting & associating materials: Plastic furniture undoubtedly looks best in a contemporary setting, with materials to match.

HAMMOCKS

This free-standing hammock is supported on a elegantly minimal frame, and should be light enough to move around the garden at will and is especially useful for gardens without any suitable trees. It should be a straightforward matter to remove the fabric from the frame for cleaning or replacement.

Characteristics: Hammocks provide the simplest and one of the most comfortable ways of relaxing in the garden, though they are far from easy to get in and out of; perhaps this is why you tend to spend a whole afternoon in a hammock, rather than just the five minutes you promised yourself! Historically, canvas was the traditional material for hammocks, but this has largely been superseded by synthetics that are far more durable. The best hammocks use ample material, and come in a variety of open-mesh weaves as well as closely woven sheets. Most are still slung at will between two stout trees, but some up-market models now come complete with their own heavy stand. While these are useful for treeless town gardens and do away with the need for trees with stout trunks, the stands can be difficult to move.

I do not really mind about colour, it is comfort that is the most important factor, but if I had to choose, I would stick to cream. A few well-chosen cushions are essential.

Uses: Relaxation, mostly for people, but cats also love them. There can be few things better than gently swinging over the long grass of an orchard in the dappled summer sun.

Construction: Secure supports are essential; a fall can be painful and dangerous. Two strong trees are probably the best choice, although you could use bolts securely fixed to sturdy posts or walls. The hammock itself should always be regularly checked for wear, and ropes or fabric replaced as necessary. This is a feature that you could certainly make yourself.

Contrasting & associating materials: If you want to be ultra-sensitive, the materials could blend with others used elsewhere. I am not too worried! An informal setting is best.

CANVAS

In my view, one of the greatest benefits of creating a beautiful garden is the pleasure obtained by relaxing in it. This scene has terrific charisma that has been achieved by combining a few simple elements: an old carpet flung on the terrace in the shadow of a fine tree, with canvas cushions tumbled around it. The view beyond is pure magic!

Characteristics: Canvas is a laid-back, easy-going material that always seems to smack of holidays by the sea, or picnics on the lawn. This is probably entirely due to childhood memories, but these things stick, which makes them all the more attractive. The material is surprisingly tough, is available in a wide range of colours and designs, and can be used for awnings, parasols or chairs, of which the best known are deckchairs and so-called directors' chairs. Both types fold up for easy storage.

Awnings and parasols have gained in popularity over the past few years, and parasols are now made in a variety of sizes, the largest able to shade a considerable area. Most have adequate methods of anchorage, but this is obviously an important consideration. Unlike the gaudy floral affairs that used to be the only kind available, many awnings and parasols are also now available in an undemonstrative buff or cream that blends well into most settings.

Beanbags also make terrific garden furniture, for dogs as well as people, and are easily made up at home using waterproofed canvas and polystyrene beads. 'The bigger the better' is the rule.

Uses: Chairs and beanbags for sitting, awnings and parasols for shade. As all are made from fabric, the scope as regards colour is considerable. This is an area where you can really inject instant and immediate interest, and then remove it just as easily.

Construction: Chairs hinge and fold in various ways, the framework normally being of timber. Although it is usually best to buy them, they are not impossible to make, if you have the time and patience. The canvas, or now rather more often, woven polyester, does wear over a period of time, but can usually easily be stripped off and re-tacked, stapled, or clamped back in place.

Canvas makes an excellent material for awnings, and these may be as straightforward as a single sheet cast over the branches of a tree, overhead beams or some other kind of framework, or as complicated as a specially manufactured structure that is rolled on a spring-loaded frame screwed on to the house wall. Parasols involve rather more intricate moving parts that slide up and down a central pole. This makes them relatively difficult to construct yourself. The material is usually stitched in position over the framework, and is similarly complicated.

Contrasting & associating materials: As with soft furnishings in the house, canvas garden furniture should be bought to blend with the setting; on the terrace, it will have a strong link with the interior of the house, so colours should be chosen with care. Apart from this, canvas furniture looks happily at home nearly anywhere in the garden: on a lawn, beside a pool, or within the shelter of a summerhouse.

Deckchairs are the most practical of chairs for storing and carrying around the garden. They are also extremely comfortable, and the fabric is easy to remove for cleaning or replacement. Be cautious about allowing children to put them up or down as fingers are easily trapped.

This composition has a wonderfully moody atmosphere! The unusually coloured parasol makes a perfect link with the colour of the building behind and has been carefully positioned over the most sheltered part of the garden.

TOPIARY

Characteristics: The art of topiary, and it is very much an art, dates back thousands of years. The skill is to clip or train virtually any kind of plant material into almost any kind of artificial shape. These can generally be divided into architectural shapes (cubes, cones, obelisks, balls, arches) and virtually any other shape (animals of every conceivable and humorous kind, as well as trains, ships, houses, cars, planes and so forth). Quite simply, the sky is the limit.

In the United States and certain other parts of the world, creeping plants, such as *Ficus pumila*, are also used to create a variety of sculptural shapes. These are grown into and over a wire framework stuffed with moss, which allows an even greater range of intricate shapes and patterns to be built up than could be achieved by clipping.

Spirals are one of the most commonly used shapes in topiary and can be straightforward to achieve. Box, used here, is one of the best plants to use as it is so simple to clip and train. The accompanying ivy softens the outline of the bowl, but care should be taken to keep it in control.

Topiary can be used *en masse* in serried ranks or as a single statement; the scale huge or diminutive; the subject serious or funny; the setting formal or informal: the choice is yours! But perhaps the most important thing is that such shapes can be created by anyone with just a little, or a lot, of imagination.

Uses: Very much as living sculpture, and almost invariably as some kind of focal point to draw the eye. Both choice and positioning have infinite possibilities; the only real limitation is the ultimate characteristic of the species involved, and the need to plant it in a position where it can develop without visually swamping the immediate area.

Construction: This is the skilled part of the job. Much topiary uses slow-growing and dense hedging plants such as yew or box (though many other plants can be also be used). An individual plant is usually trained around some kind of framework that will outline the shape required. The branches will be carefully tied into the frame, and clipped so that the form slowly takes shape. The process may take a couple of seasons or many years, depending on the size and complexity of the finished article. The frame is often removed once the shape is complete, and any further trimming will depend on the eye of the gardener. (It has to be said that strange mutations sometimes develop after a while!) For simpler shapes, such as an obelisk or lollipop, the plant is often allowed to grow up freely, with or without a stem, and trimmed against a template when the time comes. As with any heavily pruned plant material, regular feeding is essential.

Contrasting & associating materials: This will depend on the style of the piece. Geometric shapes in a fine old garden will look perfect set among sweeping lawns and gravel paths, while something far more contemporary, and perhaps humorous, will look at home in a hi-tech setting of concrete, decking and pre-cast paving.

Topiary on a large scale is an art form, albeit one that requires careful and regular maintenance. There is considerable rhythm and movement in this composition, which draws the eye down the central path and on into the garden beyond the archway. Gravel makes an excellent foil to clipped plants.

MOSAICS

This most elegant of green rooms is filled with colour and textural interest. The seats are both delightful and durable, and you could have a great deal of fun choosing colour-coordinated cushions. The floor is gorgeous and echoes the dramatic walls at a higher level, while the free-standing furniture has also been well chosen.

This is a relaxed and clever arrangement that really works, demonstrating how drama can be used to create stunning effects. Vibrant colour makes a strong design tool, and this mosaic bench matches the wall perfectly. The tangled planting with its wayward roots has become an integral element of the overall pattern.

Characteristics: The golden age of the mosaic was in Roman times, when both floors and walls, inside and outside the home, were often worked with great skill and panache. Mosaic is characteristically built up from small pieces of coloured and glazed tile, either specifically made for this purpose, or from broken fragments. The work is carried out in much the same way as a painting, except that the individual pieces, of which there may be many thousands, are stuck in position. Today, the mosaic is undergoing something of a revival, and as a garden feature it has great potential, both in terms of visual appeal and of durability.

Uses: As a decorative element on the floor or walls. Mosaic can be used to line a summerhouse, a grotto, or a swimming pool; the best examples create stunning pictures or designs, not just a bland application of a single colour throughout.

Construction: If you have a creative eye, you may well be able to undertake the design and construction yourself; if not, there are a number of artists who specialize in the field. As the end result is exceptionally durable, make sure that you choose or create a pattern that you like; it will be visually demanding, and with you for a long time!

Pieces of mosaic about 12mm/½in sq are first assembled in large batches of the same colour. The pattern or picture is drawn out on the wall or floor before work starts, and the individual pieces are then either set in a cement grout or applied with a waterproof adhesive. Once the work is complete, the joints, which should be as small as possible, are finished by grouting the entire surface. It is of course essential that the vertical or horizontal surface to which they are applied is perfectly sound, and that the mosaic is constructed from materials that are frost-proof.

Contrasting & associating materials: Mosaics are highly individualistic, but can be designed to blend into either a classical or contemporary setting, with materials to match.

ACKNOWLEDGEMENTS

The publisher would like to thank the following photographers and organizations for their kind permission to reproduce the photographs in this book.

1 Jerry Harpur; 3 left Marcus Harpur (Jonathon Baillie); 3 right Michelle Lamontagne/Garden Picture Library; 4 Ron Sutherland/Garden Picture Library (Christopher Bradley-Hole); 5 Ron Sutherland/Garden Picture Library (Designer : Michelle Osborne); 6 John Glover; 7 S&O Mathews; 8 Ron Sutherland/Garden Picture Library; 9 above Marion Nickig; 9 below Christian Sarramon; 10 left Christian Sarramon; 10 right Jerry Harpur (House of Pitmuies); 11 left Jerry Harpur (Designer: Bruce Kelly, NY); 11right Andrew Lawson; 12 Christian Sarramon; 13 Claire de Virieu, 14 The Garden Picture Library; 15 left Charles Mann 15 right Marianne Majerus; 16 above Gary Rogers; 16 below Marianne Majerus; 17 Annette Schreiner; 18 left Marianne Majerus (Heale House); 18 right Jerry Harpur (Bourton House, Gloucestershire); 19 Beatrice Pichon-Clarisse (Designer: Guy Laine); 19 right Andrew Lawson (Courtesy Frank Cabot, New York); 20 Brigitte Thomas; 21 Tim Street-Porter/Elizabeth Whiting & Associates; 22 Jerry Harpur(Jean Melville-Clark); 23 above Jerry Harpur(Designer: Jason Payne, London); 23 below Neil Lorimer/Elizabeth Whiting & Associates; 24 Jerry Harpur(Designer: Jim Matsuo, Los Angeles, CA); 24 Tim Street-Porter(Designer: Luis Barragan); 24 left Andrew Lawson(Courtesy of Frank Cabot, Quebec); 26 Andrew Lawson(Courtesy of Nancy & Bill Frederick, Delaware); 27 Jerry Harpur(Designer: Robert Watson, Christchurch, NZ); 28 S & O Mathews; 28 Marianne Majerus(Fairhaven Garden Trust); 29 S & O Mathews; 30 Jerry Harpur(Designer: Fred Watson, Alton, NH); 31 Brigitte Thomas; 32 Gary Rogers; 33 left Marianne Majerus; 33 right Gary Rogers; 34 Jerry Harpur(Wyken Hall, Suffolk); 34 Jerry Harpur(Designer: Mark Rios, Los Angeles, CA); 35 Andrew Lawson(Courtesy of Nancy & Bill Frederick, Delaware); 37 Charles Mann; 38 Steven Wooster(Designer: Di Firth); 38 Elizabeth Whiting & Associates; 39 fritz Von der Schulenburg/The Interior Archive; 40 Christian Sarramon; 41Karl Dietrich-Buhler/ Elizabeth Whiting & Associates; 42 Steven Wooster(Designers: Bev & Ken Loader); 43 Lanny Provo(Zen Buddhist Garden, Kyoto, Japan); 44 Jerry Harpur(Wollerton Old Hall, Shopshire);44 Andrew Lawson(Designer: Jim Keeling); 45 left Gary Rogers/The Garden Picture Library; 45 right Gary Rogers; 46 left Jean Pierre Godeaut(Gilles Clement); 46 right Jerry Harpur('Dolwen' Cefn Coch, Llanrhaeder-ym-Mochnant); 47 left Andrew Lawson(The Crossing House, Cambridge); 47 right Andrew Lawson; 48 right Fritz Von der Schulenburg/The Interior Archive; 49 Karl Dietrich-Buhler/Elizabeth Whiting & Associates; 50 Gary Rogers/The Garden Picture Library(Designer: Henk Weijers); 51 Claire de Virieu; 52 Wildlife Matters; 53 Geoffrey Frosh; 54 Andrew Lawson; 55 above Jerry Harpur (Designer: Beth Chatto, Elmstead Market, Essex); 55 below Andrew Lawson; 56 Gary Rogers; 57 left Marianne Majerus; 57 right Andrew Lawson(Courtesy of Mrs Thomas Hall, Maine); 58 left S & O Mathews; 58 right Marianne Majerus(George Carter); 59 Mark Fiennes; 60 left Clive Nichols(Designer: Anthony Noel); 60 right Clive Nichols(Whatton, Leicestershire); 61above Charles Mann; 61below Vincent Motte; 62 left Marianne Majerus; 62 right Jerry Harpur('Dolwen' Cefn Coch, Llanrhaeder-ym-Mochnant); 63 left Gary Rogers; 63 right Jacqui Hurst; 64 left Marianne Majerus; 64 right Gary Rogers; 65 Vincent Motte; 65 Marijke Heuff; 66 left Jacqui Hurst; 66 right The Garden Picture Library; 67 left Gary Rogers; 67 right Marianne Majerus(Artist: Jean-Pierre Raynaud, Gallerie Beaubourg, Vence.); 68 Charles Mann(El Zaguan, Santa Fe Historical Society, Santa Fe, NM); 68 S & O Mathews; 69 Jerry Harpur(Designer: Edwina von Gal, NY); 70 Wildlife Matters; 71 left Neil Campbell-Sharp; 71 right Andrew Lawson; 72 left Andrew Lawson; 72 right Lanny Provo(Yates Jungles Garden); 73 Jerry Harpur(Designer: Jim Matsuo, Los Angeles, CA); 74 Fritz von der Schulenburg/ The Interior Archive; 75 above Fritz von der Schulenburg/The Interior Archive; 75 below Marijke Heuff(Walda Pairon); 76 above Andrew Lawson; 76 below Gary Rogers; 77 Lanny Provo(Owner: Dennis Jenkins); 77 Christian Sarramon;